DAVID RABINOWITCH

Do not be misled if I often call up images
of the past. Even what is past still exists in
the fullness of its presence if instead of
focussing on content we focus on intensity.

Rainer Maria Rilke

To my mother, Ruthe Calverley Rabinowitch, 1917-1998

DAVID RABINOWITCH

Josée Bélisle

With the collaboration of
David Carrier,
Donald Kuspit,
Catrina Neiman
and David Rabinowitch

Musée d'art contemporain de Montréal
National Gallery of Canada

David Rabinowitch

An exhibition organized by the Musée d'art contemporain de Montréal in collaboration with the National Gallery of Canada, Ottawa. This exhibition is presented at the Musée d'art contemporain de Montréal from 24 April to 5 October 2003 and at the National Gallery of Canada from 6 February to 30 April 2004.

Curator: Josée Bélisle, Curator of the Permanent Collection, Musée d'art contemporain de Montréal

This publication has been produced by the Direction de l'éducation et de la documentation du Musée d'art contemporain de Montréal and the Publications Division of the National Gallery of Canada.

Managing Publisher MACM: Chantal Charbonneau
Chief, Publications Division NGC: Serge Thériault
Design: Fugazi, Montréal
Printing: St. Joseph Print Group, Ottawa

The Musée d'art contemporain de Montréal is a government corporation funded by the Québec Department of Culture and Communications and receives financial support of the Department of Canadian Heritage and The Canada Council.

© Musée d'art contemporain de Montréal and
  National Gallery of Canada, Ottawa, 2003

Legal Deposit: 2003
Bibliothèque nationale du Québec
National Library of Canada

Acknowledgements
David Rabinowitch; Catrina Neiman; docteur Paul Mailhot; Peter Blum Gallery, New York; Guy Gogeval, Musée des beaux-arts de Montréal; John R. Porter, Musée national des beaux-arts du Québec; Yves Lacasse, Musée national des beaux-arts du Québec.

National Library of Canada Cataloguing in Publication Data

Bélisle, Josée.
David Rabinowitch.

Exhibition catalogue.
Issued also in French under same title.
Co-published by: Musée d'art contemporain de Montréal.
Includes bibliographical references.
ISBN 0-88884-771-8

1. Rabinowitch, David, 1943- – Exhibitions.
I. Carrier, David, 1944- . II. National Gallery of Canada.
III. Musée d'art contemporain de Montréal. IV. Title.

N6549 R33 A4 2003   709'.2   C2003-986000-0

Distribution
Arts Books Canada
372 Ste. Catherine O., Suite 230
Montréal, Québec, H3B 1A2
Telephone: (514) 871-0606
Fax: (514) 871-2112
www.ABCartbookscanada.com
info@ABCartbookscanada.com

Contents

Foreword

Marcel Brisebois, C.M., C.Q.
Director, Musée d'art contemporain de Montréal

As the director so clearly indicates in his foreword, the exhibition *David Rabinowitch* is directly in line with the programming of the National Gallery of Canada and consistent with its mission – classic reasons for mounting such a show. But I would venture to say that the strongest justification for exhibiting David Rabinowitch's works further reason, is an experience I had some months after we decided to hold such an exhibition at the Musée d'art contemporain. When I learned that the French government had commissioned David Rabinowitch to restore and refurbish a venerable Romanesque church, Notre-Dame-du-Bourg, the original cathedral of the town of Digne in Haute-Provence, I made a trip to see the site for myself. Passing through the narthex, I was greeted by two volunteers, senior citizens, who praised the work of the sculptor, unknown to them, whose efforts had literally brought the church back to life. Their awareness of the artist's intent, their comprehension of his methods and their capacity to understand his strategy and the symbols he used were easily a match for my questions and silenced any doubts I might have had about the place of new sculpture by a Canadian artist in such a setting. Their excitement was so contagious that friends accompanying me, for whom the Romanesque aesthetic has a particular appeal, were swept away by an enthusiasm I had not realized contemporary art could inspire in them.

That experience would in itself have been sufficient to convince me of the value of a show devoted to David Rabinowitch, whose work is already represented in the collection of the Musée by 28 drawings and three sculptures. The exhibition, organized in collaboration with the National Gallery of Canada, where it will subsequently be presented, is designed to emphasize the depth and coherence of an artistic process that is well known and appreciated in both North America and Europe, particularly Germany and France. While the works that grow out of this process are undoubtedly marked by spareness and rigour, the serenity they convey is as much a spiritual attribute as their austerity.

I would like to thank the National Gallery of Canada and its director for their very warm support of this project. The Musée d'art contemporain is particularly grateful to David Rabinowitch for his whole-hearted and consistent collaboration, and also wishes to pay tribute to the work of the exhibition curator, Josée Bélisle. We extend greetings to all the visitors who may find nourishment for their contemplative vision in these works: may they feel the same enthusiasm as did my guides in the cathedral in Digne.

Pierre Théberge, O.C., C.Q.
Director, National Gallery of Canada

David Rabinowitch is one of the most eminent Canadian sculptors of the 20th century. Together with the Musée d'art contemporain de Montréal, we at the National Gallery of Canada are delighted to present this major survey of his work. Rabinowitch is internationally renowned for his large-scale steel sculptures and related works on paper, in which he wrestles with such central conditions of being as gravity, perception, space and time. In his sculptures, the artist represents these abstract ideas by exploring relationships between shape, mass, thickness, pattern, solid and void. By choosing to work horizontally rather than vertically, by setting his constructions directly on the floor or ground and by incorporating multiple points of view, Rabinowitch challenges traditional notions of sculpture. His is an innovative approach both to the work of art itself and to the viewer's experience.

The exhibition showcases an array of sculptures, drawings and prints produced between 1963 and 1995. While Rabinowitch has made works mainly for gallery and museum spaces, he has also made pieces for public sites including the refurbished Notre-Dame-du-Bourg, a Romanesque church in Digne, Haute-Provence. The artist's interests are diverse, ranging across not only art and architecture but also science and philosophy. At a young age, his father introduced him to Spinoza's *Ethics.* Later he read Darwin's *Origin of Species* and Hume's *Treatise of Human Nature,* which influenced his artistic practice, as did his studies in science and English literature at the University of Western Ontario, where he obtained a B.A. in English literature in 1966.

We are grateful to the lenders as well as to the talented writers involved in the project, including the exhibition curator Josée Bélisle from the Musée d'art contemporain de Montréal and American art critic and historian Donald Kuspit. Their insightful essays are complemented by contributions from David Carrier and Catrina Neiman. We are also indebted to David Rabinowitch for his generous collaboration.

The absence of doubt lends no certainty.[1]

David Rabinowitch, 1963

The Experience of Vision:
Observations on the Work of David Rabinowitch

Josée Bélisle

The planar masses produced by David Rabinowitch, which at first sight seem compact and austere, have quietly but authoritatively asserted themselves in the realm of sculpture for nearly forty years. The same holds true for his extensive series of drawings – specifically the paradigmatically titled *Construction of Vision* begun in 1969 – which offer a concise examination of the particular relationship between discrete linear, ovoid and circular elements and their precise placement within the vast, bare plane. However, because they stem from an obvious economy of visual means and a rigour tinged with a certain classicism, these works draw us, quite literally and willingly, into the patient exercise of the act of observation. "The restoration of vision is the ambitious enterprise proposed by the artist,"[2] writes Alfred Pacquement – a visual counterpoint, we would add, to "the music of the spheres"[3] mentioned by Whitney Davis.

Rabinowitch's aesthetic project is utterly original and, in some respects, unique. From a very early age, he immersed himself in the writings of Spinoza, Einstein and Kant,[4] among others. He developed a way of thinking that leaned toward dialectics and refuted dogmatic absolutism, whether historical, philosophical or aesthetic. It is revealing,

moreover, that one of his most ambitious projects to date, the *Tyndale Constructions*, a series of plaster wall works begun in 1974, is dedicated to William Tyndale, whom the church of England condemned to death in 1536 for translating the Bible, yet whose labours formed the basis of the 1611 King James Bible version. Rabinowitch questions and challenges visual "certainties"; he proposes convincing sculptural and drawn objects, the apprehension of which entails experiencing multiple points of view at the same time as it implies the impossibility of reducing the perfectly open complexity of their construction to a single reading.

In the experience of contemplation and the deliberate reduction of formal vocabulary, certain aspects, or significant fragments, of universal knowledge paradoxically and meaningfully materialize. Observant viewers, while essentially exercising the free will of appreciation and interpretation, may be able to confirm their understanding of the work through the indications contained in the titles – some carefully descriptive and objective, some paying tribute to leading figures of science, philosophy or the arts. The clear conception and incisive quality of execution of Rabinowitch's works are brought out in the detailed nomenclature that lists their attributes and characteristics. However, it is not simply a matter of blindly and symbolically applying this matrix of information to the works' actual nature – information is not the same as knowledge – but rather of using it as an investigational instrument.

The notions of instrument and instrumentation are essential to the artist, who turns to them not only to calibrate his constructions and structure his drawings, but also, and above all, to place the person at the core of the reality of the work. Certain drawings in the *Construction of Vision* series, executed between 1973 and 1977, as well as the first *Tyndale Constructions – in 6 Panels and 2 Scales (Sculpture for Carlo Bergonzi)*, 1975-1976, and *in 2 Panels and 2 Scales (Sculpture for Carlo Bergonzi)*, 1975-1976, – respectively built at the P.S.1 art centre in Long Island and The Clocktower in New York in 1976 (and subsequently destroyed), are dedicated to the Cremona violin maker Carlo Bergonzi. The reference suggests that the artist is making with his own hands (or having master craftsmen make) an "instrument of vision" that is actualized in the presence of the observer determined to discover the many subtleties of the circles' attributes – ellipses in some of the drawings – their variations and contrasts with the rectilinear elements (and their resonances).[5]

Conceived in 1965 and 1966, and in some cases fabricated decades later, the *Gravitational Vehicles* constitute a seminal corpus in Rabinowitch's work. These complex vertical metal assemblages, made of hot and cold rolled steel, zinc or forged iron and dedicated, in turn, to Pascal, Mendeleev, Descartes, Archimedes, Newton, Galileo, Kepler, Plato, Giordano Bruno and Einstein, among others, are anthropomorphic in conception and re-situate the sculptural object in the field of gravity and in the context of theories of mechanics and physics. "It must be acknowledged, in my opinion, that the rise of physics has exerted nothing less than a cataclysmic impact upon the imagination of the modern artist," Rabinowitch said in 1990.[6]

"Dialectical and ironic machines,"[7] the *Gravitational Vehicles*, originate in both the opposition that is assumed between art and science and their unexpected synthesis. In the way they underscore reciprocal relations between experimentation and theory, they are somewhat akin to a form of "abstract intuition"[8] that is not unrelated to the notion of content. These ingenious models, whose morphology draws upon an interpretation of Frege's distinction

between sense and reference[9] as well as of Kant's transcendental aesthetics and logic,[10] describe various relations between mass (a solid, suspended central core) and volume (a structure built to hold it), and between the perceptible sense of a central conic element and the circumstantial stages in the revelation of its frame of reference. The coexistence of inertial mass and gravitational force within these instruments of knowledge and demonstration may refer to celestial and perceptual mechanics as envisaged over the centuries by the different scientists alluded to. These works explicitly embrace certain Constructivist episodes in art history, as described by Whitney Davis: "Tatlin's monumental allegory of human construction… the novel metrics and special apparatus Duchamp simultaneously built into and depicted in the *Large Glass*… Giacometti's *Boule suspendue*…"[11]

In *Pascal's Instrumentation*, 1965, constructed in 1992, Rabinowitch deftly positions in the volume of a room the configurations of masses and voids that run throughout his work. "One of the few *Gravitational Vehicles* which is based on a mathematical theorem,"[12] as Catrina Neiman wrote in 1991, this sculpture is founded on a circular, triangular and polygonal deployment of metal rods rising conically in space, as if to defy the laws of gravity that a solid, steel element suspended from the ceiling acts to reconfirm. The different axes and the two irregular hexagons at the base and top set up a construction whose specific geometry initially resists the eye's understanding, and they generate surprising dynamics of reciprocity and relativity between the forces and materials interacting in the gravitational field and the perspective plane.

The principal cycles of Rabinowitch's work might suggest that the artist broaches concerns that are diametrically opposed. What could the conic planes, the metrical sculptures, the plaster-panel *Tyndale* works with their carved, concentric rings, the refined drawings of *Construction of Vision*, the more profuse, "expressive" *Drawings of a Tree* and those of German Romanesque churches have in common? These major groups, developed more or less at the same time, during periods spanning several decades from the 1960s to the present, do not reflect any eclecticism, however, and in fact constitute a fundamental project investigating the modes of representation through drawing and sculpture – one that is in no way aimed at resemblance but directly concerns the principle of knowledge. Rabinowitch proposes the conscious experience of perception and recognition by presenting dichotomous polarities that have always preoccupied him: what he calls internal and external conditions, container and contained, straight and curved line, vertical and horizontal, the density of mass and quality of light, solid and void. For each cycle, he elaborates a system, or rather a set of considerations and properties, that marks out the conditions of experience and facilitates, over time, the synthesis of the act of seeing and that of recognizing and knowing.

"The family of conics is an emblem for the equivalence between empirical and rational truths."[13] To Rabinowitch, the figure of the cone embodies the continuum of all possibilities. "The cone is the dialectical solid, i.e., the one which possesses a totality of oppositions."[14] Each of its sections gives rise to different configurations: circle, ellipse, parabola, hyperbola. "The convention, which has interested me since childhood, of a round thing changing its appearance to become an elliptical thing as the result of the angle of perception was a foundation of much of my thinking."[15] At the root of such works as the *Wood Constructions*, 1966, the *Tubers*, 1966-1969, the *Phantom Group*, 1967, and subsequent drawings such as *Construction of Vision*, since 1969, as well as numerous important sculptures including *Sequenced Conic Section Constructions in 4 Orders*, 1984-1987, and *Sequenced Conic Constructions in Three Domains*, 1995, this fluid figure, capable of transformation, becomes the elemental constituent of constructions that are all very precisely differentiated.

Metrics may be defined as a system of spatial measurement, but it also refers to prosody and the concerted articulation of diverse components. The planar masses of the *Metrical (Romanesque) Constructions*, begun in 1973, are subjected to configurations, divisions and perforations that initiate relations of scale and rhythmics. The notions of measure and quantification play a part in our perception of distance and expansion. As in the Conic Planes, horizontal extension is here confronted with the restrained verticality of the thickness of the plates made evident by the cuts and drillings, and with the obvious verticality of the viewer engaged in the act of apprehension. These constructions suggest "a survey of the world" (in Whitney Davis's words[16]) through the exactness of the proportions and cuts, arising out of the artist's exploration of German Romanesque churches, begun in 1971.

In the tradition of the master builders and master craftsmen, be they masons, carvers, blacksmiths or carpenters, David Rabinowitch accepts only "fundamental"[17] materials, including steel ("steel is in our society one of the basic materials"[18]) along with certain carefully selected varieties of wood, as we will see in connection with the *Wood Constructions*. And, as he demonstrated in sober yet striking fashion in his interior works (stained glass windows, tapestry, and ecclesiastical furniture and objects) for the Romanesque cathedral of Notre-Dame-du-Bourg in Digne, France, from 1993 to 1998, he may also use copper inlays in the stone of the floor (a sign and word system "indicating the dissemination of the word of God from the original Hebrew to present-day French"),[19] transparencies of clear or acid-treated glass, onyx (in the tabernacle), and so on. For Rabinowitch, using natural or appropriate materials supports "the relationship between an individual human being observing something and the way it is constructed."[20]

Of the *Wood Constructions* conceived between 1966 and 1967, *Open Quasi-Conic Wood Construction, III (Poplar)*, 1966-1967, constructed in 1989, is one of the most imposing. Rabinowitch drew some forty of these works, each meant to be made from a particular variety of wood.[21] The poplar sculpture, executed by Tadashi Hashimoto with the assistance of Satoru Igarashi, unites the conic and the rectilinear in an asymmetrical form. It merges vertical thrust and horizontal deployment in an open structure in which the rather dark, cavernous inner space contrasts with the outer shell, an impressive light, hollow volume. Without any real beginning or end, the sculpture, which totally resists a single viewpoint, works according to a quantum of essential dualities: planes and volumes opening and closing, top and bottom, back and front, etc. In this sculpture, the constants of perspectival vision and gravitational forces are applied to create an entity that can be decoded on a human scale, through rotational movement, stasis, and the passage of time.

In a different and furtive way, *The Phantom: Conic (Elliptical) Plane with 2 Double Breaks, I (Convergent)*, 1967, places an elliptical plane with folds and deflections close to the floor (height: 7 cm). Persistently eluding assertion, this steel conic section, which "formally" allows a gradual apprehension from nothingness to fullness, expresses the temporal, transitional nature of the different viewpoints and perceptions. *Round Plane in 4 Masses and 2*

Scales (with Elliptical Hole), II, 1971, built in 1989, represents a convincing example of manifest and effective simplicity. The clarity of its reading – a circular mass, slightly off the floor (13 cm), divided into four unequal parts by two subtly curved axes – is based on obviousness together with its continual refutation, which occurs as soon as the viewer moves. The angles formed by the cut lines change, and the markers of scale provided by the two holes – one orbital, in the centre of the plate, and the other, part of a vector running from one of the cut lines – energize the inevitable inertia of this dense, compact raw material. With its complex appearance, the more hybrid *Conic Plane in 9 Masses and 3 Scales*, 1978, reveals and affirms the verticality of the cuts, made all the more apparent by the two interior voids and the multiple holes in different scales. The irregular contour of the masses and the harmony of their assemblage make the work a viable construct.

The act of observation, a premise of both creation and apprehension, is inherent in Rabinowitch's practice, whether in his sculpture or in his drawing, which constitute two independent pursuits. Particularly evident in the *Drawings of a Tree* series begun in New York in 1972, the insistent gaze captures and conveys, without the least mimesis, the essence of the tree, the relationship between the plant motif, the vital quality and the countless facets of their representation. It is not a question of imitating nature, but rather of projecting onto it, in the rapid strokes, the vigorous gesture and the tonal, even tactile values, the conditions of experiencing a living being. From the beech tree drawn in *Central Park*, 1972, to the elms of *Tompkins Square Park*, since 1994, convincing archetypal impressions come to life on paper, favoured fragments of a landscape reframed in the truth of shadow and light. In addition to charcoal and pencil, Rabinowitch uses a beeswax and ground-charcoal-based medium which he invented in 1973, when he was drawing the Ottonian Romanesque churches. This medium allows variations in intensity and an expressive monochrome effect in which the line merges with the plane, the ligneous motif (or what remains of it) dominates the background and the dialectics of positive and negative is established through transparencies and overlays. The artist's first drawings of Romanesque architecture formed the basis of the cycle *Ottonian Construction of Vision,* begun in 1980. Taking up the whole area (or sheet) of paper, the earliest works define details or portions of the interior and exterior architecture, while retaining the austerity and eloquence

of the proportions and emphasizing the quality of the relationship between the fenestration, the ethereal light and the physical presence of the components. The later, more abstract, works continue to favour a vertical sheet layout in which the axes and masses materialize in through reduction and the almost repetitive nature of the strokes.

The question of colour and its properties gives rise to remarkable, distinctive developments in David Rabinowitch's work. "Color, inescapably it seems to me, has a distinct reality accordingly as it pertains to different domains of expression,"[22] he says. *The Construction of Vision Color Property Drawings*, 1972-1975, demonstrate an intelligence and refinement of the gaze wholly concentrated on the particular qualities of colour in its inclusion within the circular forms and its actualization in the linear axes. Carefully calibrated and sparingly used, colour nevertheless plays a decisive role. "A property of color constitutes our index for scale judgment insofar as it can sustain a division between external and internal properties."[23] The *Collinasca Cycle* (1992) is above all an essay on colour, a repertory of primary, irreducible geometric figures,[24] subjected to hierarchical sequences which Rabinowitch recognizes as related to the spirit, if not the letter, of Mendeleev's periodic table. Of all the cycles and series that punctuate his work, this ambitious cycle of woodcuts, potentially totalling 288 prints, forcefully and precisely reiterates the artist's mastery of the clarity of the figure viewed as an elemental expression. The first part of the cycle – twelve prints – examines the most fundamental form, the circle – coloured, concentric, paired or alone. These large, human-scaled prints continue, through the medium of woodcut, the rudimentary gesture of carving used in the *Tyndale Constructions*. The simple repetition of the circular motif suggests, beyond all the symbolic connotations it may convey, that there is always more to see than there appears. And that out of a study of classification, division, subdivision and assemblage, we come to the experience of knowledge.

However brief, these observations on various aspects of the work of David Rabinowitch attempt to define its contextual scope and unique aptness. These visually polyphonic yet sober and measured works formulate significant, fundamental relations between sculpture, architecture and science, as well as between drawing and philosophy, and even music. Commenting on the *Tyndale* work in his studio (*Sculpture for Timaeus*, 1976-1978), and its five

Tripartite III (For Catrina), 1994
Beeswax and charcoal on paper
154 x 101.5 cm
Collection of the artist and
Annemarie Verna Galerie, Zürich
Photo: Thomas Cugini

components, the artist explained: "I considered this distribution as being comparable to the hands, the parts of the body most continually within our vision. The sculpture was named *Timaeus* because it was he who said that the universe was created after the manner of a 'living creature.'"[25] Rigorous and luminous, the art of David Rabinowitch appeals to the forces of nature and, in its mental and visual constructions, proposes new models of order and harmony.

Translated by Susan Le Pan

*Tyndale Constructions in 3 Scales
(Sculpture for Timaeus), 1976-1978*
Artist's studio, New York
Photo: Jerry Thompson

1. David Rabinowitch, "Selected Notes, from the Sketchbooks, 1963-1970," *David Rabinowitch. Skulpturen 1963-1970* (Bielefeld: Karl Kerber Verlag, 1987), p. 273.

2. Alfred Pacquement, preface to *David Rabinowitch. Constructions métriques 1988-1991* (Paris: Éditions du Jeu de Paume/Réunion des musées nationaux, 1993), p. 7.

3. Whitney Davis, "Pacing the World: David Rabinowitch's *Metrical Constructions*," *David Rabinowitch. Constructions métriques*, p. 42. This essay also appears, slightly modified, in Whitney Davis, *Pacing the World: Construction in the Sculpture of David Rabinowitch* (Cambridge, Mass.: Harvard University Art Museums, 1996), chapters 6 and 7.

4. The monographs and catalogues devoted to the artist, including the three publications just cited, all mention this fact in their biographical notes.

5. Thomas Lawson comments on this in "The Sculpture of David Rabinowitch 1968-1978," *David Rabinowitch: 25 Skulpturen von 1968 bis 1978* (Krefeld: Museum Haus Lange Krefeld, 1978), p. 25: "Bergonzi... is referred to because David Rabinowitch feels he too is making an instrument which becomes fully realized only when adequately used in the context of vision."
    Catrina Neiman further notes: "The reference is both to the making of the sculptures by hand and to the notion of the observer as performer, in particular to the point that only in the playing is the instrument alive in all its resonant potential." "A New Order of Sculpture," *David Rabinowitch. Tyndale Constructions in Five Planes with West Fenestration. Sculpture for Max Imdahl 1988* (New York: Barbara Flynn/Richard Bellamy, 1990), p. 67.

6. David Rabinowitch, "Remarks on the *Gravitational Vehicles*," *David Rabinowitch. The Gravitational Vehicles* (Vienna: Galerie nächst St. Stephan/ Rosemarie Schwarzwälder / Paris: Galerie Renos Xippas, 1991), p. 59.

7. Ibid., p. 66.

8. Ibid., p. 62.

9. Ibid., pp. 62-63.

10. Ibid.

11. Whitney Davis, "The Sense of a Frame of Reference: David Rabinowitch's *Gravitational Vehicles*," *David Rabinowitch. The Gravitational Vehicles*, p. 23. This essay also appears in Whitney Davis, *Pacing the World*, chapter 3.

12. Catrina Neiman, "Catalogue of *Gravitational Vehicles*," *David Rabinowitch. The Gravitational Vehicles*, p. 119.

13. David Rabinowitch, *David Rabinowitch. Skulpturen*, p. 275.

14. Ibid., p. 276.

15. Excerpt from a letter from David Rabinowitch to Erich Franz, April 1985. Quoted by Catrina Neiman in "The Construction of Vision," *David Rabinowitch. The Major Sequenced Conic Sculptures* (Chemnitz: Städtische Kunstsammlungen / Stuttgart: Daco-Verlag Günter Bläse, 1995), p. 15. This text also appears in Neiman, "A New Order of Sculpture," p. 60.

16. Whitney Davis, *David Rabinowitch. Constructions métriques*, p. 29.

17. David Rabinowitch, quoted by Catrina Neiman in "A New Order of Sculpture," p. 83.

18. Ibid.

19. Translated from the explanatory leaflet, Cathedral of Notre-Dame-du-Bourg, Diocese of Digne, 1998.

20. David Rabinowitch, quoted in "A New Order of Sculpture," p. 83.

21. Three others have been built: one in basswood, *Basswood Tube*, 1966-1969, and two in pine, *Open Pine Piece*, 1966-1967, and *Closed Pine Piece (Inclined Closed Elliptical Plane)*, 1966-1969. Charles Soilleux built the first two.

22. David Rabinowitch, "*On the Collinasca Cycle*," *David Rabinowitch. The Collinasca Cycle* (New York: Peter Blum Edition, 1993), [p. 5].

23. David Rabinowitch, "Selected Notes 1971-1975," *David Rabinowitch. The Construction of Vision Color Property Drawings* (Warsaw: Gallery of Contemporary Art Zacheta, 1999), p. 41.

24. David Rabinowitch, *David Rabinowitch. The Collinasca Cycle*, [p. 5].

25. Quoted by Catrina Neiman in "A New Order of Sculpture," p. 78.

All that is meant in science by the "necessity" of the causal
relation is that given the conditions the result follows, and not
otherwise. In other words, if you assert the existence of the
conditions, you are logically bound to assert the existence
of the result.[1]

A. E. Taylor, *Elements of Metaphysics*

Dialectical Necessity:
David Rabinowitch's Sculpture

Donald Kuspit

Working within the constructivist tradition, as he himself has acknowledged, David Rabinowitch has produced an enormous oeuvre of geometrically intricate sculptures. Donald Judd singled out Rabinowitch as "the exception... in the general decline" of art, signalled by the re-emergence of Expressionist painting in the eighties.[2] Pure form took second place to the human figure. Interest in the human condition displaced interest in the essentials of art, which had been the major concern of the most innovative modern art. Existential images masked aesthetic stagnation, even though the aesthetic drama inherent in autonomous art had existential import. Judd observed that in this situation – as he saw it – it was inevitable that Rabinowitch's art would be "neglected." But it was also neglected because Rabinowitch stubbornly refused to associate himself with the New York Minimalism – the new artistic fashion when Rabinowitch began working in the sixties – in which Judd himself was an exemplary figure. He stood out as a maverick – a genuine nonconformist – within the new mainstream, and thus was not fully attended to.

In what amounts to a statement of purpose, Rabinowitch made it quite clear why he thought "that works included under this term [Minimalism] were based on assumptions, attitudes and intentions opposed, even contradictory to mine. They... were primarily conceived as objects" and as such did not, "with any degree of conviction, take into account relations to observers." They were not concerned with "the gravitational field," they assumed a "divide between concept and thing" or "thought and body," they were not interested in such fundamental properties of "perceptual acts" as "the distinction of right and left," they were not "explorations in time," all of which point to the fact that "Minimalism was interested in neutralizing reality, not investigating it"[3] – which is what Rabinowitch's works do. The question is how they do so, more broadly, what it means to do so.

Rabinowitch tells us at once: it means to realize that "body-mind distinctions... [are] utterly fantastic" – that it is a "delusion" to believe that there is a body substance that is distinct from a mind substance, as Descartes thought. As Rabinowitch says, he sides with Spinoza and Hume whereas the Minimalists side with Descartes and Locke. As he implies – correctly I think – this makes his art thinking advanced and original and that of the Minimalists old-fashioned and retardataire, however superficially "progressive" and novel. "Spinoza's greatness as critic of Descartes" is that he demonstrated the "falsity" of the "pervasive and insidious... presumption of the existence of two substances" basic to Descartes's thinking. Thus Rabinowitch, who is philosophically inclined, addresses, through art, the age-old issue of the body-mind relationship, arguing, as post-Cartesian thought does, that it is a mistake to separate them, that is, to assume that they are opposed and perennially at odds. We differentiate them for linguistic and cognitive reasons, but experientially they are indistinguishable: where there is body there is mind, where there is mind there is body. We murder to dissect, Wordsworth famously wrote, and we murder reality by theoretically dissecting it into body and mind, a reductionist division that simplifies and superficially clarifies at the expense of experiential depth and complexity. Rabinowitch thinks that in art "the only way to right the blunder" – however intellectually inevitable it may be – is to invent construction which "presupposes [perceptual] acts as determinant, that is to say, which formulates these as the conditions of [sculptural] objects."[4]

For Rabinowitch it is the "temporal aspect of perceptual acts" that exposes the fallacy of the mind-body bifurcation, for it is in and through lived time that their unity is perceived. It is the reality of time that Minimalism ignores, and to ignore the reality of time is to create a mindless body, which means an object that appears to exist apart from the temporal condition that makes it possible, and for that matter apart from the spatial condition of existing in a gravitational field. Minimalism naively assumes a quasi-timeless "groundless" object, when in reality the object exists as such only in and through the spatial-temporal field that is the ground of its being. Thus Rabinowitch's constructions, however modernist, that is, however deeply invested in the three-dimensional medium that is material sculpture, are not standard abstract art – a manipulative apotheosis of the formal facts implicit in the material medium, to use Clement Greenberg's terms, in order to achieve a sense of aesthetic purposiveness – but rather abstract art that articulates, with epiphanic intensity, the necessary conditions of being a real object in space-time. For Rabinowitch the sculptural object, whatever its aesthetic elegance – and Rabinowitch's have an unexpected gracefulness (a quality

that marks the highest art, according to Vasari) – epitomizes the fundamental conditions that make its existence possible, and as such is a kind of devious tautology.

Rabinowitch's artistic originality has to do with his philosophical originality, in contrast to what he calls the "majority of what passes for sculpture," which lacks artistic as well as philosophical originality because it "follows the [Cartesian] error obediently" or uncritically. Rabinowitch struggles to demonstrate in the medium of art what philosophers have struggled to demonstrate since Spinoza: that mind and body (concept and thing) are one "substance," to use Spinoza's term. Rabinowitch's way of doing this is to make a construction which incorporates its necessary conditions, thus making them evident – for example, a construction which is as flat as the ground on which it rests – while showing that such primitive planarity is not a sufficient condition for the construction, that is, does not in and of itself make for the mind-body unity which is the work of art. The necessary condition of flatness determines the formal purposiveness of the object, but it has to be invested with mindfulness, as it were, to become art. To do so is to finesse the condition's necessity – to outsmart the spatial condition while acknowledging it. Mind means structure – structured flatness, indeed, different levels of primitive material flatness, which is what we see in Rabinowitch's *Box Trough Assemblages*, 1963 and *Fluid Sheet Constructions*, 1964 – and structure means constructing difference within an undifferentiated continuum, without undermining the experience of continuum. (Rabinowitch notes that in both series "a real distinction cannot be maintained between thought and body, whereas with works classed as minimalist this distinction is basic.")

The resulting work is what might be called a dialectical continuum. An undifferentiated continuum is a naive unity, while a dialectically differentiated continuum – a continuum whose differentiated parts form a unity which remains uncannily terse despite being an extensive continuum – is intellectually sophisticated as well as expressively resonant. The successive parts – and succession is simultaneously temporal and spatial – are *petites perceptions* within the infinitely extendible continuum that is the sculptural work. Its continuity is constrained, as it were, only by the material and cultural conditions of its making – evident in the local character of its particular parts – as well as by the artist's desire, which correlates

Box Trough Assemblage,
13 Troughs and 6 Sheets, 1963
10 x 500 x 900 cm (approx.)
Collection of the artist
and Hans Knoll Gallery, Vienna
Photo: Eduard Rahs

with the continuum. That is, the seemingly impersonal continuum becomes the medium of personal desire, which means that its extension or inhibition becomes an emblem and metaphor of the state of desire. Thus the sculptural continuum suggests emotional flexibility and fluidity as much as its limits suggest self-control and self-determination.

I think this is the point that Rabinowitch was making when he declared that "the constructivist tradition I'm involved with is essentially bound up with that of the Northwest Coast tradition," a notion that would no doubt seem strange to most artists – particularly the European ones – who have worked in that tradition. But Rabinowitch points to "the totem poles," in which "all light construction is concerned with taking out mass in a linear fashion,

in a very limited number of depths" – which could be a description of his own constructions. So is the rest of the statement. "And individual elements – the eye or the beak – are conceived as parts that are nevertheless whole entities, placed together with other such whole entities. The eye/beak/wing construction is a collection of parts that are wholes.... The genius of this art is how these constructions link up with one another and yet are all kept separate. They get their unity, finally, from the pole," that is, the extensive continuum which is the pole and which they serve to structure. Like a totem pole, a Rabinowitch construction is a disrupted continuum, as it were, continuously unfolding while divided within itself and thus seeming to infold – a doubly perpetual process and reality (to refer to Whitehead's theory of their inseparability), and as such an accretion of real geometrical parts forming a

Crest Pole – Saga'Ween's Pole
Carved by Oyai
North American Indian – Northwest Coast – Nisga'a
Photo: courtesy of the Royal Ontario Museum, Toronto

peculiarly organic whole. The reference to eye/beak/wing suggests the primitive, elemental impact Rabinowitch hopes his sophisticated geometrical constructions have – and which they do have. That he usually constructs his abstract linear "totems" of metal planes – wing-like, although perhaps more like the wings that fell from Icarus rather than the wings on which an eagle and angel soar – has to do with the fact that he lives in an industrial rather than pre-industrial culture, such as the Northwest Coast culture, where having a sharp hunting eye (an eye as sharp as a beak) is a necessity of survival.

Let's get down to a few particulars (which is all I can do in the limited space of this essay). In the *Box Trough Assemblages* the planar continuum embodies the flatness of the ground that is its necessary condition, but the trough finesses the flatness by its edges and openness, which are continuous with the open space and walls of the room. At some places the trough is covered or enclosed, while at other places it is wide open, suggesting the contradictoriness of space. Thus a certain tension – a seemingly unresolvable dialectic between two and three dimensions as well as openness and closure – is created, making the sculpture something more than the logical result of its flat condition. The tension is also evident in what Rabinowitch calls "the primitive directional oppositions – right/left hand (observational condition of extension) and upper/lower (observational condition of the base)" conveyed by the "congruent displacement" of the parts into which the continuum is divided. They are perhaps most crucial to the sculpture's aesthetic effect, at least to my mind's eye, for while clearly measured, suggesting that the work is a logical construction, they occur eccentrically, giving the work an illogical appearance. The sense (or is it illusion?) of discontinuity within continuity – of discrepancy within consistency, contradiction within uniformity – makes for an experience of lived time and space. This makes the sculpture a revelatory experience of its own terms – of reality, for its terms are the universal conditions of all reality. Rabinowitch dialectically ruptures the seemingly straightforward causal relation between the conditions for the work and the work itself, suggesting that it does not inevitably and mechanically follow from the conditions however informed by them. This implies that the work has a certain intellectual autonomy however much it is a revelation of fundamental reality. To state this another way, I am arguing that Rabinowitch's sculpture defies its own premises while

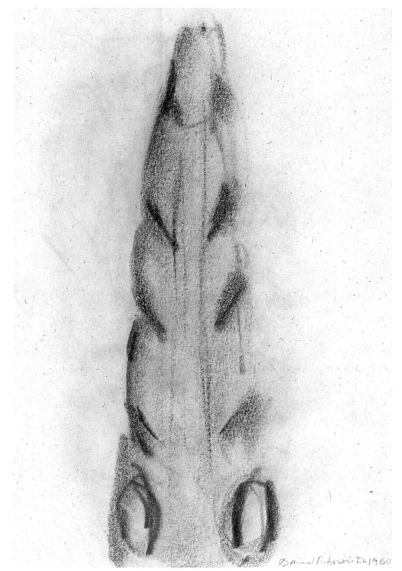

acknowledging their inescapability, in effect incorporating them in stoic acceptance. His sculptures are simultaneously closed and open systems, which is why they seem uncanny and suspenseful – self-sufficient in their contradictoriness.

Long Field Construction, 1964 is a continuum that rises and falls like a wave, making it seem systematic and eccentric at once. *Tyndale Constructions in 5 Planes with West Fenestration (Sculpture for Max Imdahl)*, 1988, an even more ingenious demonstration of discontinuity within continuity – a continuity constructed of subtle discontinuities (concentric circles carved in three depths – think of what Rabinowitch said about the totem pole – on different masonry walls of a gallery space, and thus subtly different perceptually) – indicates the importance of

site for Rabinowitch. Rabinowitch's most brilliantly subtle works – perceptually and cognitively subtle masterpieces, at least for me – are the various *Conic Wood Constructions*, 1966 and *Sectioned Mass Constructions*, 1970. Rabinowitch has said that "The family of conics is an emblem for the equivalence between empirical and rational truths," which brings together the empiricist idea that "necessitation means observed uniformity of conjunction" and the rationalist idea that "necessitation means implication."[5] He has also said that "The conic sections, directly expressive of the solid, perfectly embody a prime motif in sculpture, viz., the translation of the dimensions into one another's terms." He also notes that "The cone has the peculiarly important property of being able to represent the continuum of all sizes."

Uniformity of conjunction and implication – one part necessarily following from the other, however much they don't follow in perception (making for the effect of discontinuity and contingency) – are self-evident in Rabinowitch's extended continuums. Two and three dimensions co-imply one another, suggesting their translatability if not interchangeability. In contrast, Rabinowitch's *Conic Wood Constructions* and *Sectioned Mass Constructions* – conic sections whose masses have also been conically sectioned, that is, the seemingly idiosyncratic "faults" in the mass are conically determined and mark conic edges – seem like concentrated or condensed rather than extended or elaborated continuums. Fluid continuum seems to have been "translated" into compact mass – and vice versa – with no loss of fluidity.

It is a unique feat – truly exceptional sculpture, to remind the reader of Judd's praise – next to which his wall-climbing extended continuums, with their uniform parts – "cloned parts," one critic cleverly called them – look simplistic, mechanical, and pseudo-intellectual. No time is necessary to grasp Judd's unsubtle principle of consistent succession. Repetition neutralizes reality, to remind the reader of Rabinowitch's remark about Minimalism, which means to deny that there is anything exceptional about it. The earthy texture, weight, and density of Rabinowitch's *Mass Constructions* and the outdoor, "naturalistic" feel of his equally epic *Conic Wood Constructions* adds an empirical vigor to their dialectical rationality that makes Judd's redundant Minimalism look limited, trivial, and impotent – unexceptional – in comparison. Judd's Minimalist entropic objects (which is what Smithson also thought they were) look like the end of the constructivist line – the decadence of the constructivist tradition in mindless regularity – but Rabinowitch's constructions, with their complicated internal relations and strange irregularity (however constructed they look spontaneous and mysterious), show that it still has life in it.

Open Pine Piece, 1966-1967
Pine wood
304.8 x 92.1 x 45.7 cm
Collection of the Art Gallery
of Ontario, Toronto
Photos: courtesy of the Art Gallery
of Ontario, Toronto

1.   A. E. Taylor, *Elements of Metaphysics* (London: Methuen, 1961 [1903]), p. 183.

2.   Donald Judd, "A Long Discussion Not About Master-Pieces But Why There Are So Few of Them Today, Part II," *Art in America*, 73 (October 1984):11.

3.   Ivona Raimonova, "A Conversation with David Rabinowitch," *David Rabinowitch: Box Trough Assemblages and Fluid Sheet Constructions 1963-1964* (Prague: Galerie Rudolfinum, 1995; exhibition catalogue), pp. 18-19.

4.   David Rabinowitch, *Skulpturen 1963-1970* (Bielefeld: Karl Kerber Verlag, 1987), p. 272. All subsequent quotations from Rabinowitch are from the section of "Selected Notes from the Sketchbooks, 1963-1970," or are notes from other sketchbooks.

5.   R. G. Collingwood, *An Essay on Metaphysics* (London: Oxford University Press, 1940), pp. 318, 316.

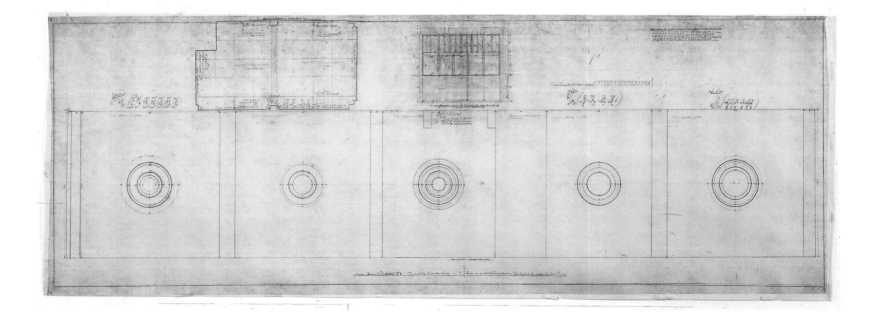

A Conversation with David Rabinowitch

David Carrier

When first I met David Rabinowitch, seven or eight years ago, it was immediately apparent that he was one of those very few extraordinarily self-sufficient artists whose work had almost nothing to do with the art world surrounding him. His sculptures, so obviously austere, deeply serious and very formally intelligent, came out of a different tradition than most 1980s art. Over the years that we talked, and the more I learned of his work, which has developed in highly complex ways for more that three decades, the more I realized the difficulty of finding adequate ways of responding to his body of work. The individual pieces themselves were highly demanding, and the internal logic of his development took time to understand. Art as entertainment; art as political critique or social commentary: these have never been of interest to him. Nor have the problems dealt with by post minimalist or post modernist American art been relevant to his achievement. His sculpture and drawing have remained firmly grounded, always, in the concerns of what might be called High Modernism. From early on, Rabinowitch had taken a great interest in philosophy; and so one of my tasks, as our relationship developed, was to return to Hume, Wittgenstein and, especially, Spinoza, to think about the ways in which the practice of an articulate sculptor might

be informed by such an intellectual background. Although deeply involved in this reading, Rabinowitch emphatically is not a philosopher-sculptor, and so one important goal was to ask in what ways the practice of his art might be informed by such reading of texts which are not much concerned, in direct ways at least, with art. His intellectual concerns, and also his working ways of thinking, were influenced by texts which he encountered early on. Born in 1943, he began reading Spinoza's *Ethics* in 1957; in 1959 he started to study Kant's *Critique of Pure Reason*; and in 1961, he started to concentrate on David Hume's *Treatise of Human Nature*, particularly its first section.

The first sculptures he thought worth preserving, the *Box Trough Assemblages* and the *Fluid Sheet Constructions*, were made in 1963 and 1964. The goal of his reading, he has said, "was always and completely bound up with my desire to engage in a program of construction that... would expose and work directly with reality. I had no wish to study philosophy as such. To me, to study philosophy is to engage in problems of philosophy. And I never did that." That statement may seem surprising, for would not philosophy take a sculptor away from direct concern with the reality of his medium? Rabinowitch's fundamental philosophical concern, I believe, is with the structure of perception as a source of knowledge, and the relation of everyday visual experience to the specifically aesthetic experiences provided by art. But this claim can only be understood by looking in some detail at his individual works, and by reflecting upon his numerous written accounts, some of them published in his exhibition catalogues. Few artists so quickly do deeply innovative work or develop in as self-sufficient a way; a proper account of his work would require rethinking the history of sculpture since the 1960s.

Canadian by birth, Rabinowitch is a part-time Manhattan resident who remains much better known in Europe than in his adopted country. As the numerous catalogues published by European museums make clear, his work is extremely well regarded for its absolutely original development of the traditions of modernist sculpture. When I knew that this Fall (1996) he would be having a show of early work at the Fogg Museum at Harvard, accompanied by a new collection of essays by Whitney Davis, I thought that it was an ideal time for an interview. It began as a discussion, and what we produced in the end was a text around that discussion, tracing some of his concerns, seeking to sketch the story of his development, and, most especially, getting him to provide some sense of his relationship to the sculptural tradition within which he has worked.

I

DAVID CARRIER: David, my introduction to your art came with the *Tyndale Constructions* at Flynn Gallery in 1988. I had the same sense of this sculpture as Jim Ackerman gives in his catalogue essay: "This work is an interior enriched, as in medieval and Renaissance buildings, by what happens on and in its walls. I see it as a chapel, a peaceful place for meditation." I wonder if this description of one piece gives a valid sense of the concerns developed in the total body of your sculptures?

DAVID RABINOWITCH: I'm happy if a piece projects for someone a meditative sense – but I've never thought about the *Tyndale* works, or for that matter anything I've made, in that way.

The *Tyndale* sculptures are very much bound up with the drawing of plans. What's your conception of the relationship between sculpture and drawing?

I would simply say that drawing is invention itself.

What significance or function did these drawings have for you?

Each finalized diagram "contains," imaginatively, a total range of attributes experienced in time and space. The plans that I preserved are each the culmination of a process.

This would appear to define a work as something more, or something other, than the physical object.

An adequate thing can never be identified solely with its physical constitution. If it is, this is a sure sign that it can not live through its own resources, such as its viewing prospects, for example, each of which may fully disclose a work's physical constitution and be simultaneously a distinct or independent thing.

This way of speaking seems to align your concerns with those of a physical scientist, with someone who develops a theory and then tests it. Is that a fair analogy; and if so, how far would you extend it?

At times I have thought of the plans as "little experiments." Making a work does presuppose an ongoing testing, a finding out of things not previously known or the continual invention and destruction of intentions. But there is no theory being subjected to tests. The "true" and the "false" are not the same things in art as they are in science.

In addition to the drawings which relate to sculptures, i.e. your sketches and plans, you also make other types of drawings. Could you say something of these?

Some of the templates, or one-to-one drawings for sculpture, I think of in some sense as another type, a kind of hybrid – simultaneously templates for works and drawings in themselves. But of the drawings not connected to works, there are in general two kinds – those that do and those that do not have reference to externals – things of the world.

Mass Works of 1968-1969
Installation view at the Fogg Art Museum,
Harvard University Art Museums, Cambridge
Photo: David Mathews

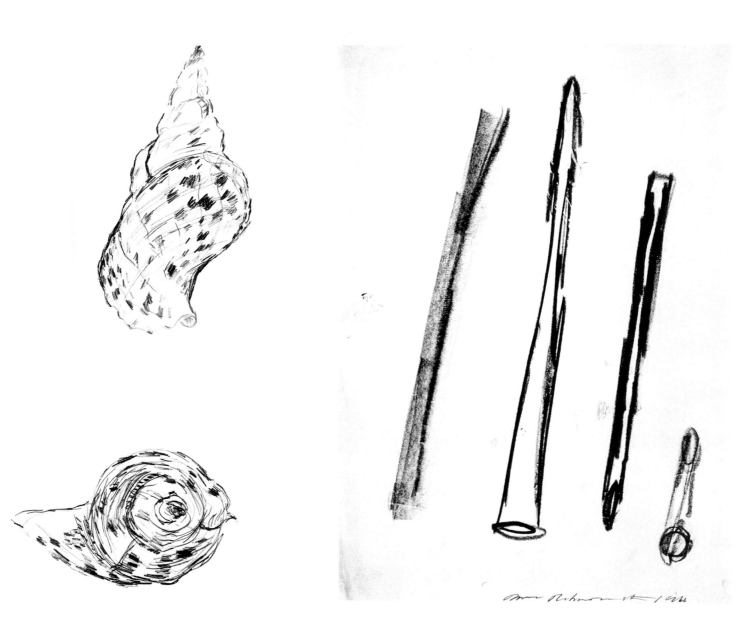

Drawings of Triton Shell, 1981
53 x 41.5 cm
Collection of Catrina Neiman

Sketches of Tubers, 1965
Charcoal on paper
21.5 x 28 cm

The drawings referring to external things were begun in 1967. I had the idea then that sculpture could be looked upon as a species synthetic of other arts (like music or architecture) and nature. I was interested in making public work that established links between aspects of nature and particular buildings. For example, the conic plane at Linz (1974-1977) associated the Bruckner Hall with the Danube.

I drew works of sculpture, works of architecture, musical instruments – each thing selected as an archetype for its kind: I made drawings after *Giacometti's Cube* (1967-1970), of the New York Kouros (1976), of the German Romanesque churches (1972-1980), of the tree in Central Park (1972-1981), of the Amati cello (1967-1968), or of the shells. I suppose I used this tripartite division partly as a pretext to draw things I wanted to contact.

And then there are the drawings that are abstract, the *Construction of Vision* drawings. These clearly are very different works.

These were conceived initially in some relation to sketches that I had made for the *Tubers* (1966). But I wanted to make drawings that had no relation to sculpture.

II

You have said that your initial way of dealing with gravity addressed the distinction between literalism and illusion. What do you mean?

The Painted Field Assemblages (1962-1963), using as a base cedar beams resting on the ground with grooves cut to contain the painted sheets, emphasized the reality of gravity. But the contradistinction between this support and the upper surfaces of painted metal represented for me a basic necessity: sculptural work must directly involve a confrontation between sensation and matter. I wanted observers to participate in both as equally real, and I took this to be a central aim of all sculpture. But many of these painted things were not adequate for me. Their importance lies in the impetus they provided for the things I made afterward in reaction, the *Floor-Wall Assemblages* and *Box Trough Assemblages* (1963). In these, sensation and matter each act as a measure for the other.

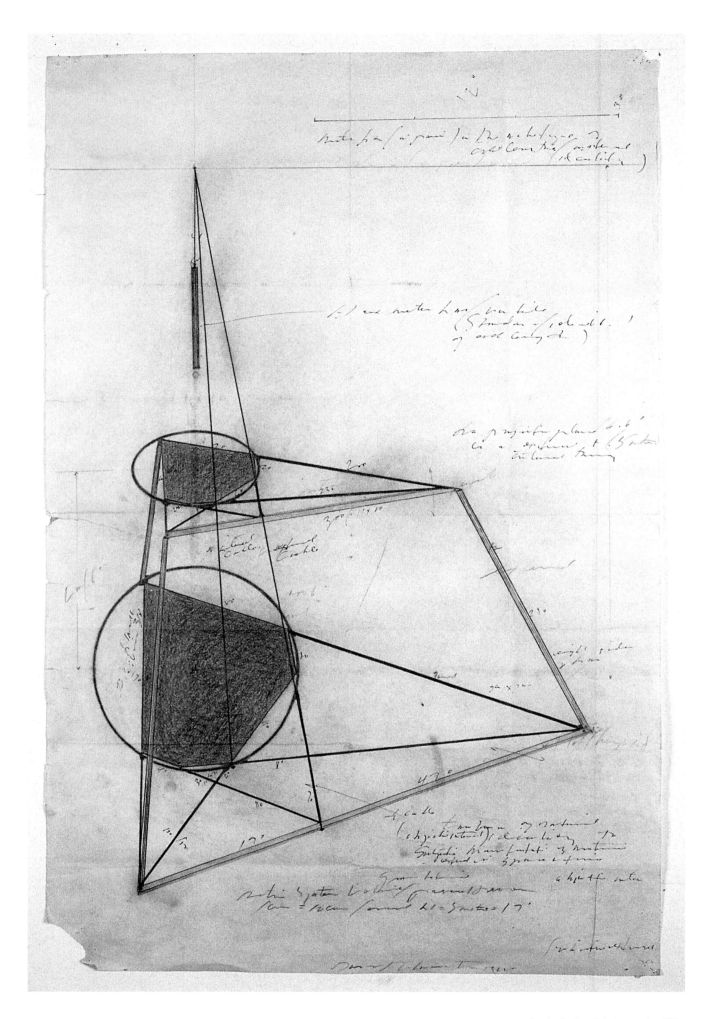

Drawing for *Pascal's Instrumentation*, 1965
Pencil and ink on paper
91 x 61 cm
Collection of the artist

What you say has, I believe, far reaching critical implications, especially in respect to minimalism, which emphasized the object-status of sculptural works. The approaches that you developed between 1962 and 1964 differ considerably from approaches developed by Minimalists.

The *Box Trough Assemblages* in particular were conceived as a critique of some properties I saw as weaknesses in David Smith's works. They were also critical of tendencies developed in England in the early 1960s.

Perhaps I can make the sense of my observation more precise by quoting Rosalind Krauss on Minimalism: "Minimalist sculptors began with a procedure for declaring the externality of meaning.... These artists reacted against a sculptural illusionism which converts one material into the signifier into another: stone, for example, into flesh – an illusionism that withdraws the sculptural object from literal space and places it in a metaphorical one" (*Passages in Modern Sculpture*, 1977).

"Externality of meaning" I suppose could refer to a focus on material conditions considered apart from private associations. Certainly the *Box Troughs* and *Fluid Sheet* pieces emphasized non- or even anti-psychological commitments to construction. So one could say that I shared a desire with the Minimalists to avoid any private meanings – whatever that means. I would have even gone so far as to claim then that the concept of meaning itself, applied to a work, is senseless. Freedom from meaning is one criterion of sufficiency.

One of your notes underscores that point: "We cannot settle any legitimate claims with respect to art in terms of meaning" (1963). Rosalind Krauss's association of an anti-illusionistic or anti-metaphorical thrust with Minimalism seems to support this thesis. She also, in reference to Minimalist work, stated that it defeated "the notion of a rigid internal armature that could mirror the viewer's own self." My sense is that you might differ somewhat on these issues.

Any notion of a private self being mirrored in a work has no place in anything I've made. A difference is that Minimalism presumes a substantial distinction between thought and experience. Thought is identified as something interior and prior, while experience is associated with *a posteriori* circumstance. The disparity becomes the focus of attention. One result is that sculpture is treated as a species of object (of whatever type) having the status of other physical structures. In my work nothing can be made of these distinctions.

Another of your notes is relevant here: "There can be no method to distinguish the properties of experience from an externally real foundation for them" (1963).

The point is that any work which operates through these distinctions tends to yield trivial experience – experience ultimately justified through meaning. That comment is directed against giving primacy to images. Image here is synonymous with meaning. A work that functions through reference to meanings uses concepts as tokens for private illumination. But this is mystification.

Whitney Davis seems to be addressing a similar situation when he suggests that for certain Minimalists "the emergence of the subject derives essentially from external conditions and relations" whereas you avoid "the seesaw in which what is apprehensible as 'specific' of 'individual' – and, most important, as continuous reality – lurches from object to subject to context to object again but never establishes what we can call a 'plane of consistency' or in Humean terms, a coherence."

The main thing is the identification of a work with a total perceptual investigation. This assumes bringing into existence what was not there before, i.e., is *not* procreative of any subject; and where there is no subject there can be no object.

III

Writing about Richard Serra's *Tilted Arc*, about the social role of sculpture, Douglas Crimp said: "Insofar as our society is fundamentally constructed upon the principle of egotism, the needs of each individual coming into conflict with those of all other individuals, Serra's work does nothing other than present us with the truth of our social condition."

The statement is right as far as it goes. Your phrase "the social role of sculpture" takes in so many complex realities that it's impossible to discuss precisely. It's also a slippery phrase. Certainly most sculpture in public spaces fails badly. Conscious attempts to make work for specifically social ends must generally be worthless. For any work to contribute to legitimate social purposes – and this is an obscure concept to begin with – it must simultaneously serve what are essentially non-social or even, as it were, anti-social ends. This is not contradictory if we think of society not as the social expression of a state, but as a constitution of individuals who demand "consciously" to take responsibility for their actions. Ultimately this idealization, let's call it a perfect anarchy, must be founded upon an antagonism to accretions of power of any one group over others. Public works that embody such recognitions are inherently critical of existent political and social norms. For works of art to have any actual social relevance they must be organized so that not only are ornamental properties continually being called into question, but the very existence of the social and physical context of a piece can be regarded as being a definite operation in that art, an operation that can itself be isolated to be judged.

Donald Judd once wrote: "The big problem is that anything that is not absolutely plain begins to have parts in some way. The thing is to be able to work and do different things and yet not break up the wholeness that a piece has." I have the sense that your view of sculpture is quite different.

Certainly one requires a work to be a plain thing. A work that has "parts" – if you mean by this, and Don did, elements that have less than a necessary relation to a thing – will degenerate. That a thing does different things is axiomatic. That the different things do not break up its wholeness – its power or intensity – is imperative. Don and I diverge in how we conceive of what makes an "absolutely plain thing." The disparity here is one of strategy, not intention. Don favoured building towards a reduction of elements which constitutes an object. I favour building towards a totality of properties which constitutes a particular. Both of us require that the particular thing be transparent to inspection, i.e., be absolutely plain. Another difference lies in how each of us thinks of what a whole thing is. Don identified this with a physical system. I identify it with conditions which are not primarily literal. Another distinction is how we treat the notion of a piece doing different things. I construct conditions bound up with properties of time. Don excluded these. By not breaking up a wholeness, Don meant preserving the literal integrity of a physical thing; for me it means the continuous regeneration of perception in respect to one thing.

IV

In his essay on the drawings you made of the tree in Central Park (*Drawings of a Tree*, Düsseldorf, 1993), Dieter Schwarz quotes a wonderfully suggestive Walter Benjamin text: "The graphic line is determined by its opposition to the surface; this opposition has not only visual but also metaphysical significance for it. The graphic line is in fact coordinated with its ground. The graphic line designates the surface and thereby determines it, by coordinating it with itself as its own ground. Conversely, there is a graphic line only on this ground, so that, for example, a drawing that covered its ground entirely would cease to be a drawing." As it stands, certainly this is a mysterious claim. How do you understand it in relation to your practice of drawing?

Benjamin's idea that line is determined "generally by its opposition to surface" is to my way of thinking another way of saying that acts of drawing are one of the co-equivalent modes of the plane of drawing – the other being the unacted upon extension of the plane. This suggests to me that perception itself constitutes a necessary mode for that plane. When Benjamin says, "a drawing that covered its ground entirely would cease to be a drawing," I believe he is obliquely affirming this.

One puzzle for me is why Benjamin speaks of this line as "designating" the surface. What exactly is the force of that particular verb in this context?

Designation connotes not only "a pointing to," but also, more important, the establishment of something. Benjamin brings this out when he links it with the notion of the line coordinating itself with its own ground. This entails a complex reciprocity. Drawing is conceived as a dynamic, enfolding two poles of reference: ground and observer. The one attribute that Benjamin does not discuss explicitly – a work's totality as a particular – is I think implied in his reference to the opposition having metaphysical significance.

32

V

I would like to turn to something that has particularly stood out for me – the way you, from the earliest to the most recent sculptures, have made frequently over short periods, in plan form or drawings, works that can be naturally classified as belonging to numerous distinct series. I'm thinking of, for example, the one-to-one scale drawings made in 1968 for the sculptures that are the first works to be conceived fully in terms of solid mass, the sculptures that will be shown in the exhibition organized by James Cuno for the Fogg Museum at Harvard. Such series of works as the *Romanesque Abutments* or the *Sided Planes with Internal Welded Members* really do, when one examines the construction drawings, show a diversity of concerns, reflected in the titles of each series.

Most of my things have been made along these lines. Even the drawings I made from the medical textbooks (1951-1952) were loosely grouped according to organ system. But I became aware of a strong necessity to work like this only after I left off painting. It had to do with a particular sense of what sculpture is. *The Origin of Species* reinforced this urge to do work that naturally falls under distinct classes. I frequently, especially in earlier times, thought of this approach as mitigating against tendencies within me which could result in a general manner or style. If one is able to make distinct works within distinct groups and simultaneously maintain a strong identity with these things, then style can count for little and the actual properties of organization in particular works and groups of work will count for a lot.

Can this approach be said to form a general methodology for you?

Altering one property can lead to a new and independent group of works, somewhat like a mutation which under rare circumstances leads to a viable species. This approach necessitates keeping a constant lookout for these kinds of possibilities. It also includes keeping a healthy distance from one's conscious intentions, keeping thought close to and expressive of complex changing experience, even to comprehending thought as non-existent apart from experience. Yes, in this sense it can be regarded as an extremely general methodology.

VI

In an unpublished note of 1969 you wrote: "The opposition between internal and external relations in one work must be a continuously reconstituted state of direct apprehension; it is the main operation for which construction takes responsibility: the opposition being reconstituted is construction's very content. And the form of construction, then, will be the means invented to affect reconstitutions of the opposition." What special pertinence does this note have to the works made between 1968 and 1969?

This note applies to much of what I've done. But it is true that the template groups for the mass works of this time were pretty much exclusively concerned with these things. That a work should somehow only involve analyses and syntheses of internal and external properties and relations – as I'm using these terms, relations count also as properties – became crucial in respect to a new recognition of how mass could be treated as the basis for construction. This was analogous to the fact that inertia and weight, though entirely distinct, are measured by the same constant quantity.

Why was it that the distinction between internal and external properties became so decisive for you in these works? What were some of the consequences?

I was led to the general distinction by confronting the problematic concerning the nature of a viable work, how it was to be constituted in experience. This had a lot to do with a work's capacity to dispel the credibility of the body-mind fantasy. To build something, the metrical properties (internal relations) of which are continuously open to an examination vis à vis changing circumstances of observation (external relations) and equally, where these relations of change become open to an examination vis à vis a work's physical constitution, just means that a work can function as an instrument to obviate the Cartesian delusion.

And here again, we come back to Spinoza's debate with Descartes – dualism. You suggested that the conception of mass you came to in 1968 was somehow analogous to the physical fact that the weight of something and also its resistance to motion, its inertia, are measured by the same constant, its quantity of substance. In what way is it analogous?

The analogy is twofold: a field of force acting on a thing is analogous to the totality of its external relations; the thing's inertia is analogous to the totality of its internal properties. The measure common to both expressions, the material quantity, can therefore be identified through analogy as a condition under which both orders are total expressions of each other. Mass in this conception is the primordial possibility for a full reciprocity between internal and external properties. Complete reciprocity obtains only so far as these are constructed as total aspects of one thing.

You wrote in another note of this period (1970) that "the esoteric and exoteric, the intrinsic and extrinsic, the static and mobile must be wrought as foundations for one another, sculpture being that expression, the power of which rests on reality and appearance being co-equivalent measures." Does this portray something similar to what you have just spoken of?

Yes, sculpture is an art that makes of its transitory attributes a whole within which to locate and determine stable properties, just as these form a complete index for the transitory attributes. It is a temporal expression as much as it is an expression against and apart from time. It can be contrived as a vehicle pitted equally against idealism and materialism and other mystifications of the world.

What you have called "the construction of total aspects" seems to have some connection to "the construction of scale" that came about in 1971 and that has had a role in almost all of your work subsequently. Was this development in fact influenced by your idea of total aspects?

A vertical plane built up through a membership of discrete drilled units distinguished in terms of classes of diameter size was indeed connected to the idea of a total aspect. The "scale construction" was intended from the first as a whole, counterpart to and independent of the plane of mass. The aspect's independence allows for perceptual operations to be generated in respect to particular indices.

You speak of judgement in regard to the two orders of the internal and external. Do not such judgements themselves affect the status of properties and relations as to whether these are to be understood as internal or external?

34

Since the scale plane is an index for judgements of the greatest generality and at the same time is built through particular indices, a hierarchy spanning the specific and the general pervades all ranges of apprehension. In this sense the distinction between internal and external properties is ultimately bound up with type and event or, to say the same thing, with universals and particulars. This finally amounts to saying that the operation of judgement coordinated to a construction of scale is a system in continuous transition generating the realities of partial and whole states.

Is this perhaps one reason that in a recent conversation with Suzanne Anna at Chemnitz in Germany you emphasized that "within this definition of objects, fantasy plays no legitimate role. Reality is limited to perceptual acts continuously being recognized for what they are in time and in space in relation to a living individual.... [A] work... is only concerned with the formation of objects of judgement, their destruction, their reconstitution. Thus a work provides for itself a ground for skeptical analysis of its existence as a totality."

The construction of scale is the basic means for an ongoing building up of syntheses and dissolutions of these. A work thus is constituted through the processes of judgement. The only way a work can stand outside of mystification and provide at the same time a sufficient foundation for freedom of experience is by laying bare its means, providing for a skeptical stance regarding its unity. Apart from this, acceptance of the unity of a thing is tantamount to acquiescence in the face of mystery.

First published in *Bomb*, No. 58 (Winter 1997), p. 61-65.

Elliptical Plane in 10 Masses and 3 Scales, I (Sculpture for Anton Bruckner and Johannes Kepler), 1974-1977
Hot rolled steel
12.7 x 330 x 1 500 cm
Collection Österreichische Ludwigstiftung und Neue Galerie, Linz
Photo: Joseph Pausch

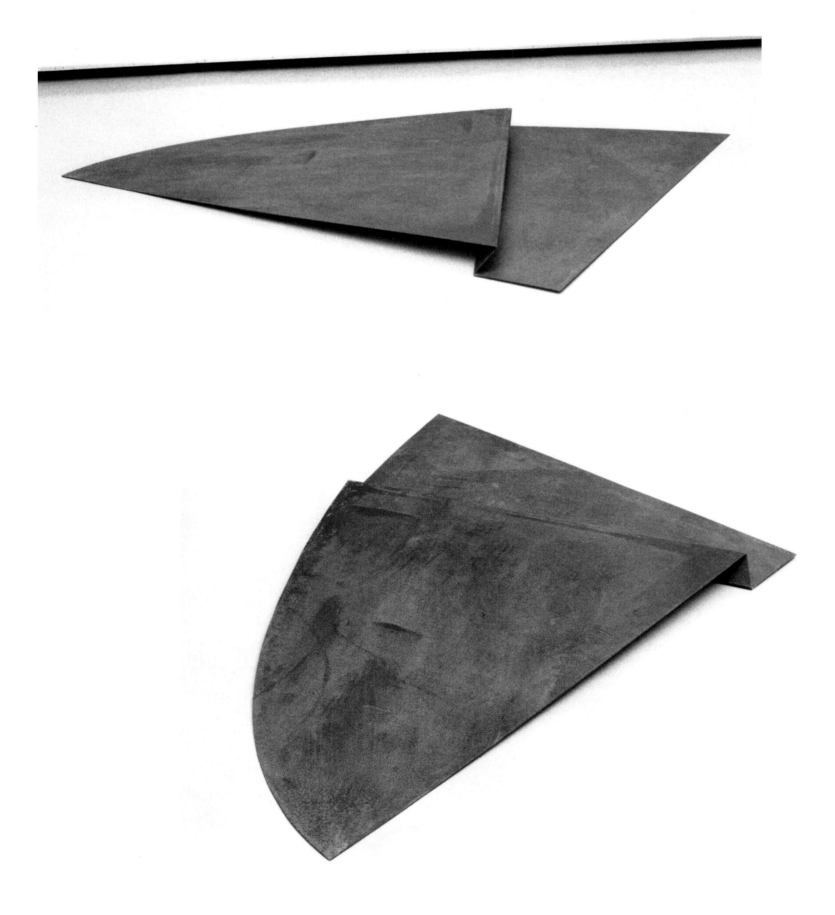

Phantom Group: Straight-Sided and Mixed Conic Plane with 1 Double Break, IV, 1967
Hot rolled steel
7 x 150 x 250 cm
Collection of the artist and Galerie m, Bochum
Photos: Catrina Neiman

The Metrical (Romanesque) Constructions Interview with David Rabinowitch

Catrina Neiman Cologne, August 2, 1982

I

Could you outline some of the background of this group of work? What considerations led up to it, before you saw the Romanesque churches?

A number of things were important for the development of the *Metrical Romanesque* works. A fundamental consideration came from the *Phantom* group (1967). Every viewing stance around each of these sculptures discloses the totality of the work's physical properties. But each of these viewing stances is also able to project a sense of the work's wholeness that is highly differentiated from all other such senses of wholeness.

Just as important was the fact that the *Phantoms'* vertical construction – the double braking operations applied to the material plane – formed the basis for this differentiation of views. The internal relations of the plane could be grasped, therefore, as a complete condition of reference for every sense of the whole of the construction, for each different total aspect the sculpture projected. Although these projections take into account the reality of perception itself, they are not any the less objectively real for that, precisely *because* each is bound up with the physical totality. Nevertheless, they are distinguished from the metric of the plane itself, which, as I said, can be thought of as the set of internal operations, that is, the intrinsic or invariant properties. All of the the "external relations," the properties subject to change, subject to stance, are secured through reference to the internal or material operations, the double vertical braking applied to the plane.

This distinction between internal and external aspects – between the actual and the perceived – you said was directly relevant to your approach to the churches.

Yes. Compared with everything else, it was the most determinant.

How, for example?

Well, any facade or elevation reflects one facet of the volumetric of the church. It expresses a part of the building's intrinsic features, its internal relations. These intrinsic properties are a visible proportion of the totality, which remains largely submerged. At the same time, the facade presents itself, from any stance taken toward it, *because* of the way it has been conceived, as a projected thing which

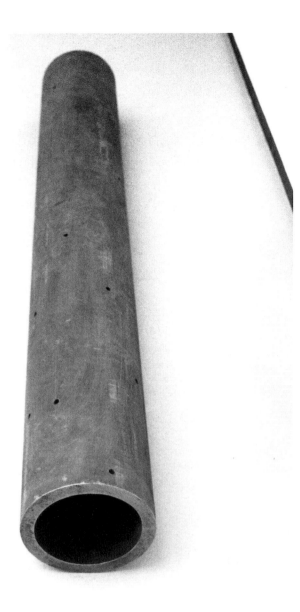

Holed Pipe, VI, 1967
Hot rolled steel
2.5 x 30 x 244.4 cm (approx.)
Collection of the artist
Photo: Catrina Neiman

can be considered a whole. And, in amazing fashion, an aggregate of such projections operates in parallel: they too form a species of wholeness. All such projected aggregates can be determined as equivalent unities, equivalent because each finds its reference in respect to the intrinsic totality. Any particular feature thereby becomes capable of being interpreted as both a part and a whole, both in the context of projected or external relations and in the context of intrinsic structure. I saw all attributes, both inside the church and outside, as participating in such reciprocal relations. But unlike the situation that I had introduced with the *Phantoms*, the church always had hidden aspects, as I said, in respect to the totality of its internal relations. This distinction was enormously important to me because it showed me that the way I wanted to make sculpture – the way I wanted sculpture to be organized in perception – could never be literally related to the way one perceived a church.

Couldn't these comparisons of how things function in perception be said to occur in any building whatever?

Technically yes, but in the Romanesque churches they happen with incomparably greater force, and this gives them an entirely different status. I mean the reciprocity of dependent and independent traits, the recessive and the dominant, or passive and active. This applies to all part-whole relations. This oscillation of reciprocal states does not, for me, occur powerfully in other kinds of buildings.

II

You've said that this reciprocity, of dominant and recessive, passive and active, is one of the kinds of interplay the vertical construction sets up in your sculptures, vis-à-vis the horizontal plane. Because this vertical, or scale, construction distinguishes the *Metrical Romanesque* sculptures from your earlier works, I'd like to hear more about its development, before going on with the churches.

The general form that the construction of scale was to follow was first developed as systems of indices for judgement, in respect to the whole material extension of a work, namely, sets of drilled units in the mass of the wall of open pipes (*Holed Pipes*, 1967) – though I didn't at the time conceive of this approach as a scale construction *per se*. The "systems" used different variational principles in their organization of classes of quantity and distribution.

4-Sided *Plane in 2 Scales, I,* 1971
Hot rolled steel
2 x 90 x 105 cm
Collection of the artist
Photo: Christine Osinski

The vertical expression was a way of directly opposing materiality to its absence or light, mass to its removal. You could say it was a way of using carving as a purely constructive means. And because of the direct association with light, the vertical unit became directly associated with acts of perception.

This was also the time when I identified, metaphorically speaking, the vertical index with expressions of "arithmetic," and its counterpart – the horizontal, material extension – with geometry. This "arithmetic expression," the index systems, would include approaches not only to counting but also measuring and sequential ordering, which meant that the organizational or variational principles I was working with depended on the most primitive manipulations of "numbers" – that is, the counting numbers, the negative whole numbers (each of the units is conceived as a discrete unit of removal). Then, in the construction of the horizontal material extension I was able to use a small selection of the inexact ratios, or measuring numbers, like π, useful to express volume and mass. At this time also I began to interpret the natural numbers as progressive sets, that is, as ordinal numbers.

This generalized approach to the use of quantity gave me great freedom to form variational principles organized in terms of degrees of complexity. I wanted an approach which could not be reduced to intentions or meanings, which would break expectations and which would involve only acts of perception.

What were the first works that used this vertical drilling as a scale construction *per se*? And how did you conceive of the notion of scale then – that is, as what kind of measuring device?

It was not until 1970 or early 1971 that I began to think of the vertical indexing systems of drilling as a true construction of scale, in works such as the *Four-Sided Mass Planes* and a little afterwards, the different groups of *Bars*. All of these had straight external boundaries, made by cutting. Like the *Holed Pipe* they had almost no internal division. But in the vertical plane holes were drilled in more than one diameter size.

I'm using the term "scale" in a fairly traditional sense, expanded to cover a wider range of implication. I didn't think of the vertical index in the *Holed Pipes* so much as an instrument or a unified vehicle, a thing. I thought of it as a system under which judgements in respect to the whole of the sculpture are indexed. But a scale construction

Plane of 10 Masses, I, 1970
Hot rolled steel
7 x 146 x 155 cm
Collection of the artist and
Annemarie Verna Galerie, Zürich
Photo: Thomas Cugini

I thought of rather as a specific tool, a measuring device, as it were, for indexing perception of the extension. The comparison of sizes identifies this instrument as an expression of multiple ratios of properties and/or relations. You could say that the major difference between a scale construction as such and the drilled systems in the *Holed Pipes* is that the construction of scale is itself articulated internally.

And then it becomes a reflexive device for examining the acts of perception that it initiates. So the construction of scale involves, for the observer, constant reference to the making of judgements and also a continual awareness of comparisons of specific differences and resemblances – all in the context of the awareness of one's own body, which is taken as the standard.

Evidently, then, the perspectival plane itself can be conceived as a kind of expression of scale, separating out the observer and the observed as constituents within a unique whole, which is in fact the way I thought of the perspectival plane when I made the *Tubers*. And it was important that the *Metrical Romanesque Constructions* also took into account the way the perspectival projections were organized in vision. This had a real influence on how I began to organize their scale construction: as a means of breaking down, of filtering, projections of the plane. The *Metrical* sculptures bring out the fact that scale at its root involves the analysis of perspective.

III

That raises another point that I wanted you to clarify. You said that the *Metrical* pieces were the first pieces to exclude curves, and that this decision involved wanting to make a group that would eliminate the vagaries that curves can set up, in perspective.

The *Metrical* pieces were the first works having internal membership that consistently did not use the conic properties. Yes: conics have an inherently indefinite quality, because of their very continuity. Definite apprehension is

*Sided Conic Plane in 6 Masses
and 2 Scales, I*, 1971-1972
10 x 300 x 205 cm
Collection of the artist and
Galerie Renos Xippas, Paris
Photo: Catrina Neiman

always somewhat lacking – apprehension of location and of the near and far. This sense of the indefinite was one of the *requirements* in the *Phantom* group and the *Wood Constructions*, where the conics are a central issue. I wanted there to use the set of conics precisely to treat these ambiguous relations.

So conic construction can never be comprehended within experience, immediately and rationally, whereas straight boundaries (internal and external), that are indexed to a construction of scale, are immediately apprehended as resolved entities. Every attribute can be definitely affirmed or denied.

I had made more recently works that addressed this distinction. The *Sided Planes* of 1970 and '71 used conics, and they had no vertical construction. Another group in 1970 used conics internally but not externally. This was a primitive method of differentiating the set of external relations from the internal. Most of the work made in 1971 and 1972, the *Sided Conic Planes*, used conic constructions together with straight cutting, and a fairly

complex set of relations in the vertical plane. So that group amounted to a generalization, in a sense, of the previous four years of work.

It could be said that I was working toward a higher degree of articulated organization with these pieces. The first *Metrical Romanesque* works came about not only because of my experience with the Rhineland churches but even more pressingly because of the need to come to terms with the indefiniteness or ambiguity which the conics presented, to work with the primitive materials of "sameness and difference" strictly in terms of properties that could be rigorously articulated, which could be strictly delimited and measured.

So you reserve the title *Metrical* for sculptures that use straight lineation only.

Yes, in regard to boundary and internal division in the material extension.

Drawings of *Romanesque Churches*, 1973
Charcoal and beeswax on paper
31 x 24 cm
Gift of Dr. Paul Mailhot
Collection of the Musée d'art contemporain de Montréal
Photos: Denis Farley

IV

What role did the Romanesque churches play, then, at this point?

When I first ran into the churches in Cologne, I knew immediately that they were exceptionally relevant to my fundamental interests. My first experience of St. Pantaleon came as a shock of recognition. I remember having the distinct sensation that I would be forced to drop everything that I was doing and concentrate on this thing.

What was the "shock of recognition"?

I wanted to investigate complex schemas in terms of metrical relations only. The churches' monumental organization, both the depths of light and the massing of members, presented itself as an absolute condition, a model for organizing a totality in terms of autonomous memberships, each of which is defined by strong internal metrical articulation. I had approached conditions resembling this but never in terms of such a high degree of "rationality."

By "rational" you mean what?

A rigorous delimiting of circumstances that can create an organization which can be contemplated impersonally.

And the churches showed me something else that was amazing, as I looked at them and drew them: that a sculpture's internal organization (in my work expressed predominantly through the scale construction) need not be in any sense less singular than the concatenation of masses. In the church, all of the fenestration, the pillars, the pilasters, any of the internal divisions of the planes of mass, function as determinant sets of metrical realities. They act as recognizable standards under which one can directly compare one thing with another. They are extremely definite. And this internal articulation is, moreover, *responsible* for each member's autonomy. A member is separate from another not only because of its properties of extension but also, and as much, because of its internal construction.

These circumstances confirmed for me that not only could the scale construction become a chief instrument of differentiation in a work but also an observational tool by which the formation of unities could take place. Autonomy of members did not mean that the members were unrelated. It meant that their relation to other members

St. Pantaleon, Cologne

St. Aposteln, Cologne
Photo: Catrina Neiman

Linear Mass in 4 Scales, I, 1972
Cold rolled steel
5 x 30 x 270 cm
Collection of Donald Judd,
Marfa, Texas

could be established through difference as well as resemblance, through the judgement – in regard to their internal properties – of classes of difference and classes of resemblance.

One would naturally compare, for instance, in your sculptures, sizes or type of distribution in the vertical construction from member to member, therefore actually "relating" the masses.

Yes. And any act of relating things could be organized through the most primitive means, in terms of difference and resemblance. Before I saw the churches, I had never seen anything that brought about, so immediately and forcefully, this need to constantly compare things and, because of the force with which it happens, the consciousness of doing so.

V

Another crucial thing is the equal importance the churches give to all elements – the exterior boundary, the interior boundaries, and the metrical organization – or what in my work would become the scale construction. I had never used such a complex set of metrical properties in the planar extension together with an equally complex set of metrical properties in the vertical construction. That is, they had never been equally important. The earliest *Metrical* works conceived of these two sets of properties in terms of equivalence. In every member there is equal emphasis on the scale construction and the boundary. This is the case even where there is no expression in the vertical plane and where the size of the member becomes itself an expression of scale.

Of all the other pieces made after 1971, i.e., of the sculptures made in more than one scale, the only other pieces that presented a true equivalence between the internal and external metrical properties were the *Bars (Linear Masses)*. In these, the bounding condition was a primitive one – these were just bars – and the internal metrics were just *as* radically simplified.

So the *Bars* are in some primitive sense an image of this metrical equivalence between the vertical and horizontal planes.

Yes, in this they are forerunners of this aspect of the *Romanesque* works.

*Metrical (Romanesque) Constructions
in 5 Masses and 2 Scales, IX*, 1973
Hot rolled steel
6 x 290 x 250 cm
Collection of Wilhelm-Lehmbruck-
Museum, Duisburg
Photo: Nic Tenwiggenhorn

45

Could that be said also of the simplified *Rectilinear Planes* of 1970-1971?

They were all essentially measuring systems, relying wholly upon sizes and lengths. They had almost no sense of the organic. That is, they had no parts; they were mostly planes of one mass, or at the most two. All organization was conceived in respect to groups of systems that could be considered equivalent to random occurrences of events.

But in answer to your question: No. In those pieces the internal construction is much more complex than the external construction. In the *Bars* they're equal, as they are in the *Metrical* pieces. I should say, in the *Bars* they're equivalently simple, and in the *Metrical* pieces they're equivalently complex.

I always wanted, since making the *Sided Conic Planes* in 1972, to have a greater control over construction in the two aspects. And the experience of the churches led me to a more systematic treatment of the equivalence of the two orders of construction.

Another important point: the early *Metrical* pieces were more primitive in some respects than later pieces are, in the sense that one member frequently has, in its scale construction, an expression which directly reflects its own horizontal conformation. In the sculpture of five masses in the studio (*Metrical Romanesque Constructions in 5 Masses and 2 Scales*, I, 1973), the location of holes of one size (the largest in this case) in a particular member reflects the unique structure of that member. They are located at the intersections of the lines drawn from the corners of the plane. So contemplating this set of holes (they're a set because they're the same diameter) is a way of contemplating the structure of the mass.

Is that the case with other masses in the sculpture?

Yes, but the vertical construction reflects the mass in different ways. What I just described is a primitive reflection. The *degrees* of reflection or coordination became for me a way of defining the degree of the member's autonomy.

The importance of this was to establish a hierarchy of independence among the members. And one could impart different statuses to the members, depending on the property, or treatment of the property, that one isolates as the basis. So in one sense, in the sculpture of five masses the large mass would have the greatest independence, but in another sense the small triangular member is more independent.

In what senses?

The large mass is the most independent if one ranks the members according to the coherence of internal organization.

By that you mean the vertical construction?

Yes. And the small mass, a triangle, is the most singular if one judges on the basis of external boundaries.

The use of different hierarchies measured in terms of autonomy is an active principle in the churches. The central eastern apse of, say, St. Gereon has, in some ways, greater controlling force than does anything else in the conformation, *if* one regards a certain property, but if one regards another property it will have less controlling force.

*Metrical (Romanesque) Constructions
in 17 Masses and 3 Scales, I,* 1985
440 x 305 x 10 cm
Collection of the Museum Würth, Künzelsau
Photos: Bern Weisbrod

VI

It should be emphasized, however, that in no sense were the *Metrical* works based as such on the churches. These sculptures are a kind of parallel set of constructions that were stimulated in some sense by the churches.

I see a Romanesque church as a unique locus, in terms of which I can freely contemplate construction – in the most general way, outside of any direct representation. I may invent an organization of elements which is equivalent in one or more respects to a certain selection of elements that make up an aspect of a church. I may interpret the manner in which the wholeness of a church operates in vision in terms of the concatenation of interior volumes, and, analogous to this presentation of wholeness, I could invent a way of organizing the unity of a work. Or it could be that this way of organizing volumes in terms of unity will evolve into a variational principle, one that can even be shared by a group of plans.

What example can you give of a "variational principle" in this context?

If I see two groups of windows associated with two cardinal directions, and if it happens that the difference between them encompasses size, distribution and number, I may create of this primary circumstance a motif that abstracts these properties grasped as a whole thing. So the variational principle in this case could be described as: seven and three [units] expressed in terms of north and south, indexed through small and large. Or a variational principle could be as primitive a thing as cardinal orientability associated with different properties, like overall proportion.

And by "variational" do you mean that you apply such a principle to different sculptures, varying its application?

It could be this, but it also could be that I apply it variously in the same sculpture.

These principles are not apparent, as such, as organizing principles, to the viewer. It is not important to you that a viewer "discover" them.

No, nor, for that matter, any relations to the church. This is merely material with which I make a work. It is in fact against my intention to have observers participate in the origins and connections which bring about a work. Means are never equated with purposes. That would be a bit like trying to associate the effect of a colour with its history of being mixed.

Every work is the result of what could be called a mixture of such principles, in fact, synthesized such that even if one could record the making, one could never establish a direct correspondence between any single variational principle and any single construction in the work.

Is this synthetic character part of what you mean when you speak of the "symphonic" nature of these works?

I would say that the symphonic character of a work *results* from this synthetic approach. Synthesis here has as much to do with the separation of diverse circumstances as with binding them. These circumstances, themselves being manifest as total, autonomous conditions, become able to communicate with one another, so to speak. It's as if one sees a work as a number of distinct characters in a drama, the whole of which is resolved through unique conflicts between individuals. The symphonic aspect reflects the church's multiplicity of articulate members and groups, the many classes of autonomous memberships that make up its totality.

48

Another reason I saw the churches as being organized symphonically was because of their ongoing synthesis of internal and external relations. This distinction underlies the whole approach to deriving a model from the churches. The domain of metrical or material properties, what I call internal relations, can be considered equivalent to the domain of reference, or objective truths. This aspect of discursive significance is analogous to what the Greeks called *diánoia*. And the domain of external relations – projective properties, coordinate with viewing stance, having to do with such conditions as the perspective plane – is then equivalent to senses of wholeness, what the Greeks called *melos*, or "spectacle." The reciprocity of these two generates a temporal dynamic, which then corresponds to what the Greeks described as *mythos* – or the unfolding. This is the life of the work.

Metrical Constructions in 13 Masses, I, 1989-1990
14 x 335 x 396 cm
Collection of the Gagosian Gallery, New York,
and Thomas Ammann Fine Art, Zürich
Photo: Jerry Thompson

Metrical Constructions in 13 Masses, I, 1987-1990
14 x 335 x 396 cm
Collection of the Gagosian Gallery, New York,
and Thomas Ammann Fine Art, Zürich
Photo: Geoffrey James

Sculptures

1. **BOX TROUGH ASSEMBLAGE (8 TROUGHS AND 6 SHEETS), I** 1963

2. **FIELD PHALANX IN 20 SHEETS AND 2 ORDERS** 1964

3. **TOOL HANDLE CONSTRUCTIONS** 1965

5. **OPEN QUASI-CONIC WOOD CONSTRUCTION, III (POPLAR)** 1966-1967

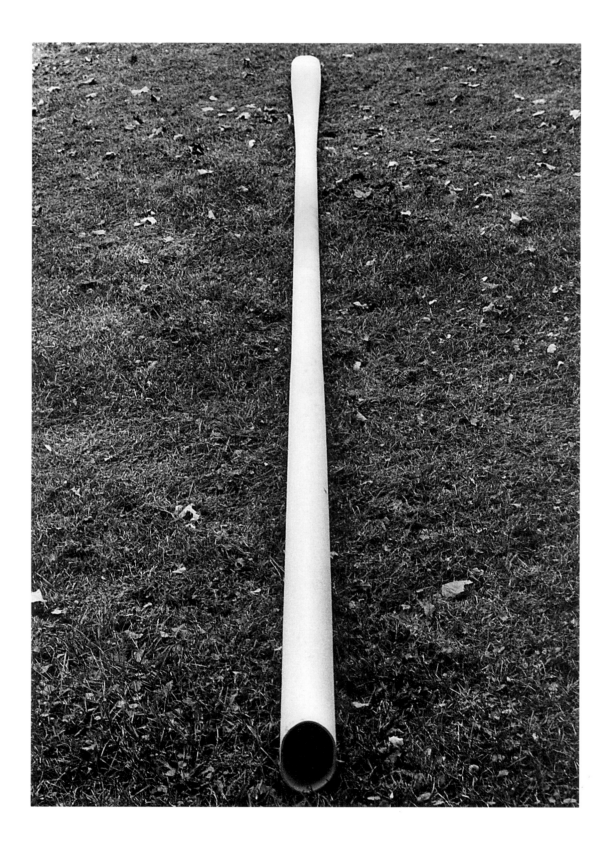

6. **ANTI-SYMMETRICAL DOUBLE TUBER** 1966-1968

7. **THE PHANTOM: CONIC (ELLIPTICAL) PLANE WITH 2 DOUBLE BREAKS, I (CONVERGENT)** 1967

8. **MODEL FOR THE SMALL POLISHED SEA: CONIC (ROUND) PLANE WITH 2 DOUBLE BREAKS, II (PARALLEL)** 1967

9. **HOLED PIPE, I** 1967

10. **HOLED PIPE, V** 1967

12. **PLANE OF 2 MASSES, V** 1969

14. **PLANE OF 9 MASSES, II** 1968-1969

15. **DOUBLE CONIC PLANE OF 4 MASSES (ELLIPTICAL), I** 1969-1971

16. **CONIC (ROUND) PLANE IN 4 MASSES AND 2 SCALES, I (WITH ELLIPTICAL HOLE)** 1971

17. **SIDED CONIC PLANE IN 6 MASSES AND 4 SCALES, III** 1972

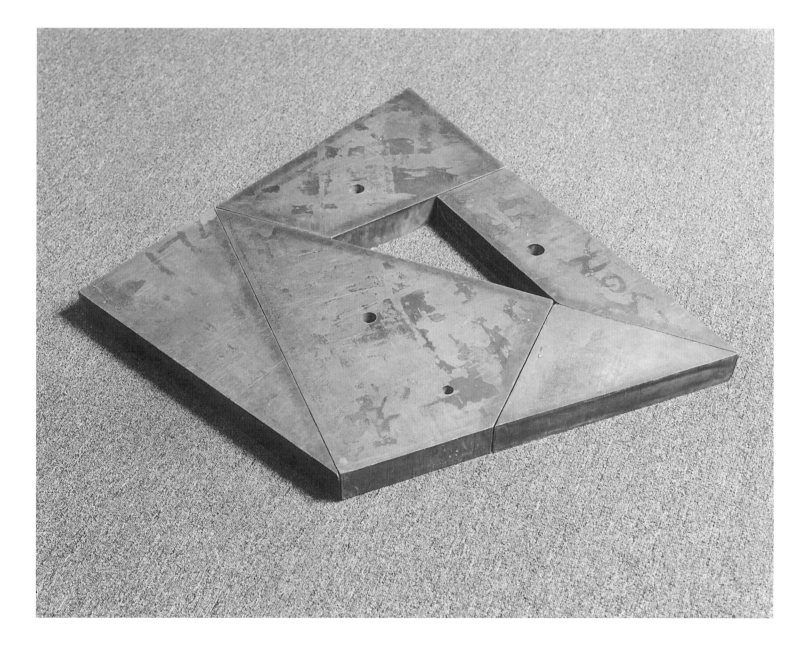

18. **SIDED PLANE IN 5 MASSES AND 2 SCALES, II (WITH INTERIOR FREE REGION)** 1977

19. **SIDED CONIC PLANE IN 9 MASSES AND 3 SCALES, I** 1978

20. **METRICAL (ROMANESQUE) CONSTRUCTIONS IN 3 MASSES AND 3 SCALES, I** 1973-1974

21. **METRICAL (ROMANESQUE) CONSTRUCTIONS IN 5 MASSES AND 2 SCALES, I** 1973-1974

22. **METRICAL (ROMANESQUE) CONSTRUCTIONS IN 5 MASSES AND 2 SCALES, II** 1975-1976

Works on Paper

23. **CONSTRUCTION OF VISION** 1970

24. **CONSTRUCTION OF VISION (DOUBLE BLUE PROPERTIES)** 1973

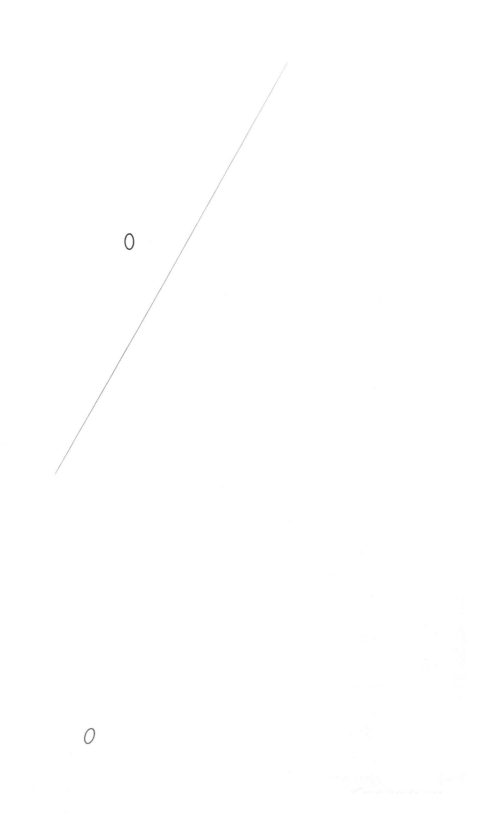

25. **CONSTRUCTION OF VISION** 1973

26. **CONSTRUCTION OF VISION (1 COLOUR PROPERTY, 4 TANGENT CONICS)** 1973

28. **CONSTRUCTION OF VISION (HORIZONTAL IN TWO SHEETS, 2 COLOUR PROPERTIES, 8 CONICS)** 1975

29.   **CONSTRUCTION OF VISION (VERTICAL IN TWO SHEETS, 3 COLOUR PROPERTIES, 4 CONICS)** 1975

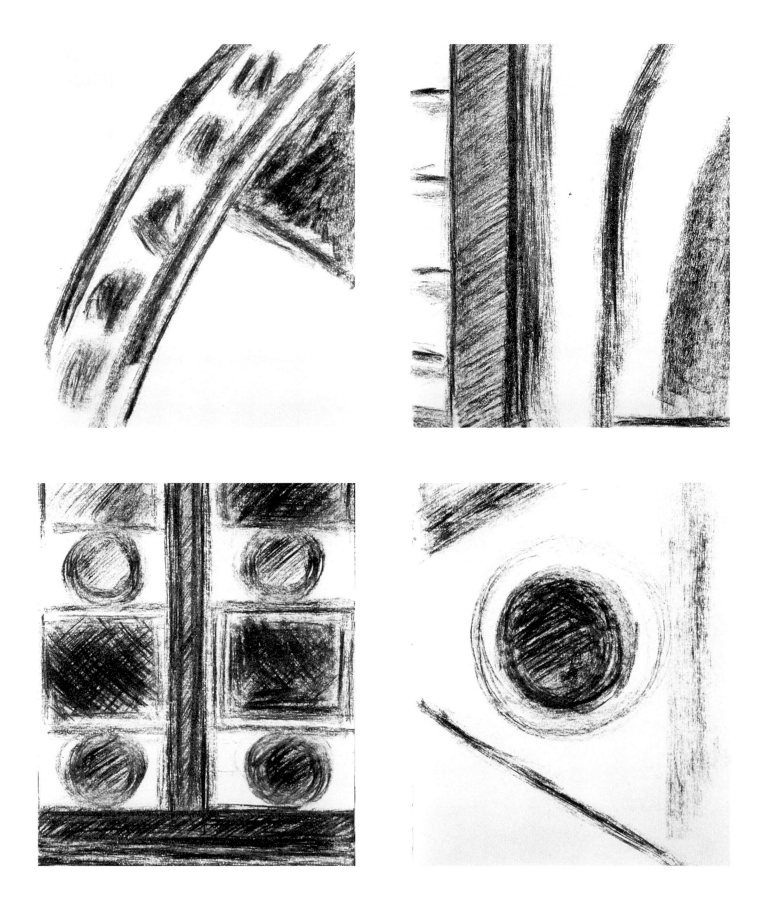

31. **DRAWINGS OF ROMANESQUE CHURCHES** 1973

32. **CONSTRUCTION OF VISION (OTTONIAN): APOSEOPEISIS** 1982

33. **CONSTRUCTION OF VISION (OTTONIAN): TANTARA** 1982

34. **DRAWING AFTER ELM TREES IN TOMPKINS SQUARE PARK, NO. 53** 1993

35. **DRAWING AFTER ELM TREES IN TOMPKINS SQUARE PARK, NO. 54** 1993

36. **DRAWING AFTER ELM TREES IN TOMPKINS SQUARE PARK, NO. 60** 1993

37. **DRAWING AFTER ELM TREES IN TOMPKINS SQUARE PARK, NO. 63** 1995

38. **DRAWING AFTER ELM TREES IN TOMPKINS SQUARE PARK, NO. 64** 1995

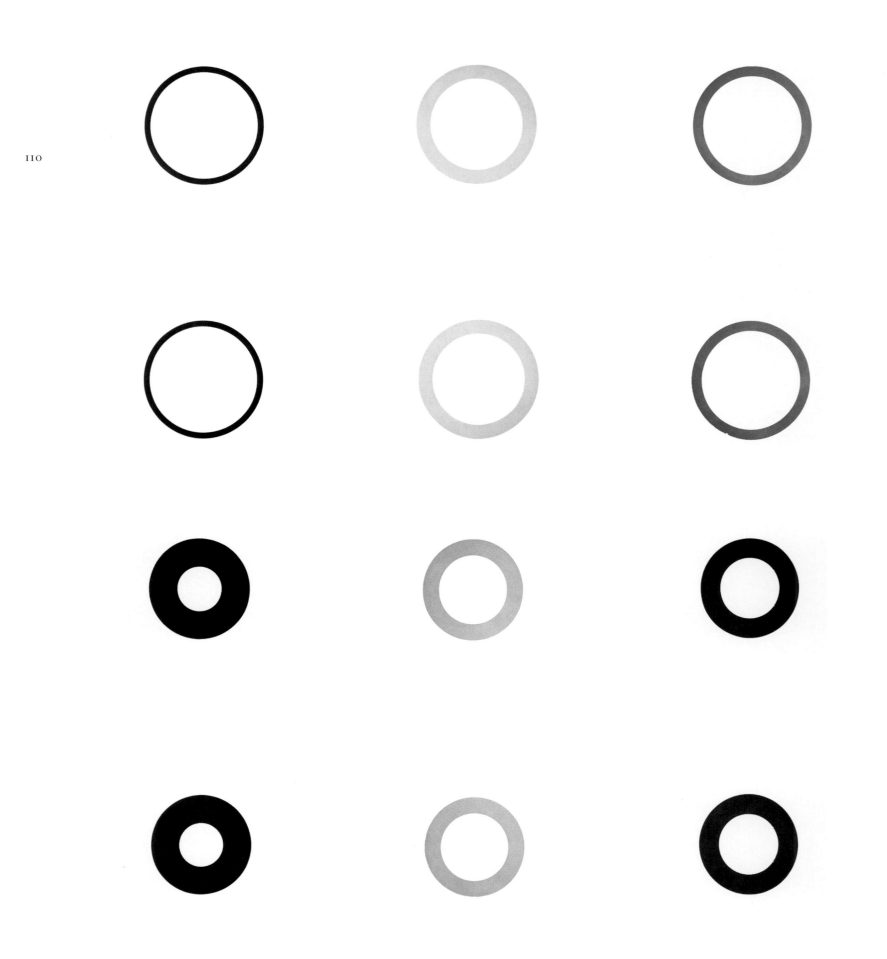

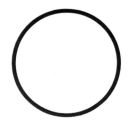
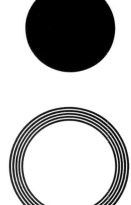

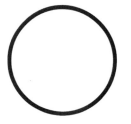

39. **THE COLLINASCA CYCLE** 1992

List of Works

Sculptures

1.
Box Trough Assemblage (8 Troughs and 6 Sheets), I, 1963
Hot rolled steel
11 x 266 x 763 cm
Collection of the artist
Courtesy of Peter Blum Gallery, New York

2.
Field Phalanx in 20 Sheets and 2 Orders, 1964
Galvanized iron sheets, 0,65 mm
20 x 300 x 800 cm
Collection of the artist
Courtesy of Peter Blum Gallery, New York
Photos: Heiner Thiel

3.
Tool Handle Constructions, 1965
Axe and pick handles (ash or hickory), 90-120 cm long,
with various operations: sliced, cut and drilled.
Mounted on wall or using table as base
Collection of the artist
Courtesy of Peter Blum Gallery, New York

4.
Pascal's Instrumentation, 1965
Steel welded and bolted with cable rigging
5 x 6 x 3 m (approx.)
Collection of the artist
Courtesy of Peter Blum Gallery, New York
Photos: Jay Manis

5.
Open Quasi-Conic Wood Construction, III (Poplar), 1966-1967
Poplar
Constructed in 1989
305 x 244 x 365 cm
Collection of the artist
Courtesy of Peter Blum Gallery, New York
Photos: Jay Manis

6.
Anti-Symmetrical Double Tuber, 1966-1968
Sandblasted aluminum
12.7 x 509.6 x 12.7 cm
Collection of the National Gallery of Canada, Ottawa
Photos: National Gallery of Canada, Ottawa

7.
*The Phantom: Conic (Elliptical) Plane with 2 Double Breaks,
I (Convergent)*, 1967
Hot rolled steel
10 x 305 x 95.3 cm
Collection of the National Gallery of Canada, Ottawa
Photos: National Gallery of Canada, Ottawa

8.
*Model for the Small Polished Sea: Conic (Round) Plane with
2 Double Breaks, II (Parallel)*, 1967
Hot rolled steel, dipped in zinc
14 x 119.6 x 103.8 cm
Collection of the National Gallery of Canada, Ottawa
Photos: National Gallery of Canada, Ottawa

9.
Holed Pipe, I, 1967
Galvanized Steel
45.7 x 243.8 cm
Collection of the National Gallery of Canada, Ottawa
Photo: National Gallery of Canada, Ottawa

10.
Holed Pipe, V, 1967
Hot rolled steel
30 x 240 x 3 cm
Collection of the artist
Courtesy of Peter Blum Gallery, New York
Photo: Christine Osinski

11.
7-Sided Mass Plane, III, 1968
Hot rolled steel
10.2 x 50.8 x 38.1 cm
Collection of the Montreal Museum of Fine Arts
Photo: Brian Merrett

12.
Plane of 2 Masses, V, 1969
Hot rolled steel
13 x 49 x 47.2 cm
Gift of Dr. Paul Mailhot
Collection of the Musée national des beaux-arts du Québec
Photo: Patrick Altman

13.
Plane of 4 Masses, III, 1969 (1988)
Hot rolled steel
13 x 75 x 36 cm
Gift of Marielle and Paul Mailhot
Collection of the Montreal Museum of Fine Arts
Photo: Brian Merrett

14.
Plane of 9 Masses, II, 1968-1969
Hot rolled steel
13 x 48.7 x 43.6 cm
Gift
Collection of the Musée national des beaux-arts du Québec
Photo: Christine Osinski

15.
Double Conic Plane of 4 Masses (Elliptical), I, 1969-1971
Hot rolled steel
3 x 83.8 x 101.6 cm
Gift of Ronald Black
Collection of the Montreal Museum of Fine Arts
Photo: courtesy of the Montreal Museum of Fine Arts

16.
Conic (Round) Plane in 4 Masses and 2 Scales, I
(with Elliptical Hole), 1971
Hot rolled steel
13 x 183 x 183 cm
Gift of Marielle and Paul Mailhot
Collection of the Musée d'art contemporain de Montréal
Photo: Richard-Max Tremblay

17.
Sided Conic Plane in 6 Masses and 4 Scales, III, 1972 (1989)
Hot rolled steel
12 x 213.5 x 183 cm (approx.)
Gift of Marielle and Paul Mailhot
Collection of the Montreal Museum of Fine Arts
Photo: Christine Guest

18.
Sided Plane in 5 Masses and 2 Scales, II
(with Interior Free Region), 1977
6.5 x 86 x 92 cm
Hot rolled steel
Gift of Dr. Paul Mailhot
Collection of the Musée d'art contemporain de Montréal
Photo: Denis Farley

19.
Sided Conic Plane in 9 Masses and 3 Scales, I, 1978
Hot rolled steel
7.7 x 144.3 x 101.4 cm
Gift
Collection of the Musée d'art contemporain de Montréal
Photos: Richard-Max Tremblay

20.
Metrical (Romanesque) Constructions in 3 Masses and
3 Scales, I, 1973-1974
Hot rolled steel
5 x 213 x 305 cm
Collection of the artist
Courtesy of Peter Blum Gallery, New York
Photos: Nan Becker

21.
Metrical (Romanesque) Constructions in 5 Masses and
2 Scales, I, 1973-1974
Hot rolled steel
6 x 183 x 244 cm
Collection of the artist
Courtesy of Peter Blum Gallery, New York
Photo: Jay Manis

22.
Metrical (Romanesque) Constructions in 5 Masses and
2 Scales, II, 1975-1976
Hot rolled steel
5.3 x 205 x 175.9 cm
Collection of the National Gallery of Canada, Ottawa
Photos: National Gallery of Canada, Ottawa

Works on Paper

23.
Construction of Vision, 1970
Pencil and coloured crayon on paper
100 x 70 cm
Gift of Dr. Paul Mailhot
Collection of the Musée d'art contemporain de Montréal
Photo: Richard-Max Tremblay

24.
Construction of Vision (Double Blue Properties), 1973
Pencil and coloured crayon on paper
101.7 x 32.1 cm (each)
Gift of Dr. Paul Mailhot
Collection of the Musée d'art contemporain de Montréal
Photo: Richard-Max Tremblay

25.
Construction of Vision, 1973
Pencil and felt pen on paper
130 x 76.1 cm
Gift of Jacques Mailhot
Collection of the Musée d'art contemporain de Montréal
Photo: Richard-Max Tremblay

26.
Construction of Vision (1 Colour Property, 4 Tangent Conics), 1973
Pencil and coloured crayon on paper
233.7 x 152.4 cm
Collection of the artist
Courtesy of Peter Blum Gallery, New York

27.
8 Constructions, 1974
Pencil on paper
127.4 x 97 cm
Gift of Dr. Paul Mailhot
Collection of the Musée d'art contemporain de Montréal
Photo: Richard-Max Tremblay

28.
Construction of Vision (Horizontal in Two Sheets, 2 Colour Properties, 8 Conics), 1975
Pencil and coloured crayon on paper
100.1 x 70.7 cm (each)
Gift of Dr. Paul Mailhot
Collection of the Musée d'art contemporain de Montréal
Photo: Richard-Max Tremblay

29.
Construction of Vision (Vertical in Two Sheets, 3 Colour Properties, 4 Conics), 1975
Pencil and coloured crayon on paper
100.1 x 70.7 cm (each)
Gift of Dr. Paul Mailhot
Collection of the Musée d'art contemporain de Montréal
Photo: Richard-Max Tremblay

30.
Construction of Vision (2 Sheets, Vertical), XXXIV, 1975
Pencil and felt pen on paper
127.3 x 97.1 cm (each)
Gift
Collection of the Musée d'art contemporain de Montréal
Photo: Richard-Max Tremblay

31.
Drawings of *Romanesque Churches*, 1973
Portfolio of 36 drawings
Charcoal and beeswax on paper
31 x 24 cm (each)
Gift of Dr. Paul Mailhot
Collection of the Musée d'art contemporain de Montréal
Photos: Denis Farley

32.
Construction of Vision (Ottonian): Aposeopeisis, 1982
Charcoal and beeswax on rag paper
287 x 203.2 cm
Purchase Saidye and Samuel Bonfman Collection of Canadian Art
Collection of the Montreal Museum of Fine Arts
Photo: Brian Merrett

33.
Construction of Vision (Ottonian): Tantara, 1982
Charcoal on paper
305 x 183 cm
Gift of Dr. Paul Mailhot
Collection of the Musée national des beaux-arts du Québec
Photo: Patrick Altman

34.
Drawing After Elm Trees in Tompkins Square Park, No. 53, 1993
Charcoal and beeswax on paper
105.4 x 74 cm
Collection of the National Gallery of Canada, Ottawa
Photo: courtesy of Peter Blum Gallery, New York

35.
Drawing After Elm Trees in Tompkins Square Park, No. 54, 1993
Charcoal and beeswax on paper
102.9 x 69.5 cm
Collection of the National Gallery of Canada, Ottawa
Photo: courtesy of Peter Blum Gallery, New York

36.
Drawing After Elm Trees in Tompkins Square Park, No. 60, 1993
Charcoal and beeswax on paper
152.4 x 102.9 cm
Collection of the Musée d'art contemporain de Montréal
Photo: courtesy of Peter Blum Gallery, New York

37.
Drawing After Elm Trees in Tompkins Square Park, No. 63, 1995
Charcoal and beeswax on paper
152.4 x 102.9 cm
Collection of the Musée d'art contemporain de Montréal
Photo: courtesy of Peter Blum Gallery, New York

38.
Drawing After Elm Trees in Tompkins Square Park, No. 64, 1995
Charcoal and beeswax on paper
152.4 x 102.9 cm
Collection of the National Gallery of Canada, Ottawa
Photo: National Gallery of Canada, Ottawa

39.
The Collinasca Cycle, 1992
Series of 12 colour woodblock prints on Japan wove paper
Edition of 20, Peter Blum Edition, New York
200 x 82 cm (each)
Collection of the National Gallery of Canada, Ottawa
Photos: courtesy of Peter Blum Gallery, New York

Biographical Notes

1943   Born Toronto, March 6.

1955   Father introduces him to Spinoza's *Ethics*, which he reads seriously over the next four years.

1956   Mother designs house in Richmond Hill, near Toronto, and it is at this time that he becomes interested in the architecture of Frank Lloyd Wright, introduced to him by students assisting his mother to draw up plans of the house.

1958   Sets up studio in basement of home. Paintings in this period influenced by Cubism.

1959   Through his mother meets painter Jock MacDonald, who introduces him to the work of painters who will most affect him: Hans Hofmann, Franz Kline, Jackson Pollock and Barnett Newman.

   Establishes studio in a barn in Kettleby, Ontario.

   Reads Einstein's book on the special and general theories of relativity written for non-scientists, and at this time begins to read Kant's *Critique of Pure Reason*.

   Writes long (unfinished) poem on the death of Giordano Bruno.

1960   Becomes involved with David Smith's sculpture, which contributes to the transition in his work from painting to sculpture. Moves studio to second barn, in Richmond Hill.

1962   Ceases painting. Makes woodblock monotypes.

1963   Moves to London, Ontario. Studies science and English literature at the University of Western Ontario.

   Sets up studio in Hyde Park, in barn and meadow loaned by Jock Metford, Professor of French. Makes first sculptures, *Painted Steel Assemblages*, partly in reaction to Smith's work.

   Visits frequently a sheet metal shop in Hyde Park, and using the brake, begins a small group of *Monochrome Wall Assemblages*. From this point, works full-time as a sculptor. Begins notes on art.

   Reads Darwin's *Origin of Species* and studies closely the first book of Hume's *Treatise of Human Nature*, which influences his thinking about sculpture. Makes *Box Trough Assemblages* and *Fluid Sheet Constructions*.

1964   Spends year working on the *Fluid Sheet Constructions*. Begins reading the poetry of William Blake.

1965   Uses various purchased objects to make sculptures (e.g., *Egypt*, *Internal Measuring Rods*, *Tool Handle Constructions*). First fabricated works are the *Gravitational Vehicles* and *Framed Wall Constructions*.

1966   Receives B.A. in English literature, University of Western Ontario. Undergraduate thesis titled *English Renaissance Exegesis on the Book of Jonah*. Marries Sheila Martin.

1966-1967   Makes *Tubers*, *Wood Constructions*, *Phantoms*, *Holed Pipes*, *Sided Pipes*, and *Sided Tanks with Holes*.

1968   Begins constructions using solid rolled plate (e.g., *Sided Masses*, *Romanesque Abutments*, *Sectioned Mass Constructions*).

1969   Makes *6-Sided Bars*, *Mass Cylinders*, *Planar Masses with Vertical Construction*. Begins *Construction of Vision* drawings, based on consideration of *Tuber* group.

1971   Develops concept of sculpture in more than one scale, using as a vertical construction the relation of sizes of drilled holes.

   Begins *4-Sided Bars (Linear Masses)*; larger *Sided Mass Planes*, with straight and curved (conic) internal and external boundaries (e.g., *8-Sided Plane in 6 Masses and 4 Scales*, collection: the Museum of Modern Art, New York).

   First trip to Europe. While staying in Cologne begins to study Romanesque churches in the region.

1972   Moves to New York. Begins drawings of beech tree in Central Park. Starts reading the *Timaeus*.

1973   Completes first *Metrical (Romanesque) Constructions*, eliminating curves (conic sections). *Construction of Vision* drawings now exclude all line construction. Crayon drawings concerned with Romanesque monuments will become the basis for later *Ottonian Construction of Vision* drawings.

1974   Begins *Sculptures for William Tyndale* and *Metrical (Rectilinear) Constructions*, e.g., *Sculpture for Piet Mondrian*. Builds *Elliptical Plane* for Project '74, in Cologne.

1974-1975 Teaches at Yale University. Receives New York State Council grant.

In *Construction of Vision* drawings begins using diptych and triptych formats; begins *Amati* series. Conceives certain drawing constructions in relation to architectural interiors (walls and fenestration). Makes wall constructions using four directions: Museum Wiesbaden and Galerie Hetzler & Keller, Stuttgart.

1975 In Halifax, Nova Scotia, makes first group of lithographs, *Test for Litho—Homage to Senefelder*, in the projected series entitled *Birth of Romanticism*.

Appointed Guggenheim Fellow.

1976 Builds three *Tyndale* sculptures in New York City, at P.S.1 and the Clocktower; builds several *Romanesque* works with Alexander von Berswordt, Bochum (e.g., for Ruhr University, Bochum). Shows three-part *Construction of Vision* drawing in War Resisters' League exhibition at Heiner Friedrich, New York. Draws *Kouros* at Metropolitan Museum, New York City.

1977 Builds with Alexander von Berswordt *Romanesque* sculpture for Documenta VI, Kassel, *Round Plane in 3 Masses and 2 Scales* in Münster, *Elliptical Plane in 10 Masses and 3 Scales (for Johannes Kepler and Anton Bruckner)* on the Danube in Linz.

Receives Victor M. Lynch Staunton Award of Distinction (Canada Council).

1978 *Tyndale* sculpture *(for Timaeus)* completed in New York studio. Builds *Romanesque* sculptures for Haus Lange Museum, Krefeld (with Alexander von Berswordt) and the Art Gallery of Ontario (with Carmen Lamanna).

1980 Begins *Ottonian Construction of Vision* drawings, based on sketches of Romanesque churches in the Rheinland. Builds *Romanesque* work with Alexander von Berswordt for *Sculpture in the 20th Century* exhibition, Wenkenpark Riehen, Basel.

1981 *Tyndale* sculpture *(for Ruthe Calverley Rabinowitch)* erected in Galerie m, Bochum. With Solidarity Lodz builds 1967 *Holed Pipe*.

1982 *Tyndale* sculpture *(for my grandfather, Horace Calverley)* built for Documenta VII, Kassel, in connection with Alexander von Berswordt. Conceives new group of *Tyndale Constructions*, many in more than one volume, using entire interior: all four directions and masonry covering total wall planes.

1983 Marries Catrina Neiman.

1984 Completes new group of *Metrical (Rectilinear) Constructions*. Begins *Sequenced Conic Section Constructions* as a formal group.

Appointed Professor of Sculpture, Staatliche Kunstakademie, Düsseldorf.

1985 Begins *Aparchai* and *Etumon* series of *Ottonian Construction of Vision* drawings. Makes first *Ceremonial Objects* at Werkstatt Kollerschlag, Austria.

Establishes second studio, in Zuidbroek, Holland.

Builds *Tyndale Constructions in 4 Scales (Sculpture for Bud Powell and Coleman Hawkins* for "Situation Kunst," Bochum (completed 1990).

1986 National Endowment for the Arts Fellowship.

1987 Builds *Sequenced Conic Section Constructions in 4 Orders* for Documenta VIII, Kassel, in connection with Alexander von Berswordt.

1988-1989 *Tyndale Constructions in 5 Planes with West Fenestration (Sculpture for Max Imdahl)* built by Flynn Gallery, New York, in cooperation with Oil & Steel Gallery, Long Island City. Begins new group of ceremonial objects (including *Ash Whale Cross* and altar) with Werkstatt Kollerschlag.

1989 In Montreal makes set of four lithographs *(Rosetta Levelling)* and monoprint using 2 stones in 2 orientations. Builds 1966 *Open Poplar Construction* with Flynn Gallery/ Oil & Steel Galleries; with Harald Szeemann, builds *Tyndale Constructions in 4 Directions (Sculpture for Mattio Gofriller)* for "Einleuchten," Deichtorhallen, Hamburg.

1990 Builds *Metrical Constructions in 13 Masses* with Flynn Gallery/ Oil & Steel, New York; five *Gravitational Vehicles* (1965) with Rosemarie Schwarzwälder, Vienna; in the Muzeum Historii Miasta Lista, Lodz, Poland, builds *Symmetrical Tyndale Constructions for the Poznanski Palace (Sculpture for my grandmother, Gertrude Rabinowitch)*; with Renos Xippas, Paris, builds early *Conic Planes* (1971-73).

1991 Begins the *Collinasca Cycle* of woodcut prints with Peter Blum in the Ticino. Builds early *Romanesque* sculpture for the Lehmbruck Museum, Duisburg, in connection with Dorothea van der Koelen, Mainz. Fabricates group of 1970 *Conic Sectioned Mass Constructions* with Annemarie Verna Galerie, Zürich.

1992 For exhibition at the Kunsthalle Baden-Baden, builds two *Conic Planes* (now at the Sprengel Museum, Hannover and the Lenbachhaus, Munich), and a *Rhomboidal Plane* (now in the Foundation "La Caixa," Barcelona), in connection with Dorothea van der Koelen, Mainz. With Alexander von Berswordt builds *Gravitational Vehicle for Kepler and Euclid*, the first hand-forged work of this group (1965) to be realized (now at the Kaiser-Wilhelm-Museum, Krefeld).

1993 For exhibition at the Galerie Nationale du Jeu de Paume, Paris, builds five *Metrical Constructions* (1988-91), in connection with Akira Ikeda Gallery, Flynn, New York, Annemarie Verna, Zürich, Dorothea van der Koelen, Mainz, and Susanne Albrecht, Munich.

Begins plans for windows and ecclesiastical furniture for the Romanesque cathedral, Notre-Dame-du-Bourg, in Digne (Haute-Provence).

Begins drawings of cathedrals St. Sulpice (Paris) and Laon, and of pre-Columbian sculptures.

Completes first group of *Birth of Constructivism* etchings, known as "Sequence for Vertov," published by Peter Blum, New York.

Begins piano works (songs) for the victory odes of Pindar.

1994 *Sequenced Conic Constructions in 4 Domains* (1984-87) is installed at Place Dauphine in Paris.

Sculptor in residence, Atelier Calder, Saché, France. Draws plans for metrical work for the ruins of the Chartreusian monastery in Liget. Completes plans for a memorial "to the Murdered Jews of Europe," Berlin.

Builds *Conic Plane*, *Sided Conic Plane*, and *Metrical Constructions* with Dorothea van der Koelen, Mainz.

Begins drawings after elms in Tompkins Square Park, New York City.

1995 Begins to draw *Kouros* at the Glyptothek, Munich.

Builds *Sequenced Conic Constructions in 3 Domains* for Museum Chemnitz (now in the Saxon Parliament, Dresden) with Dorothea van der Koelen, Mainz. Builds *Box Trough Assemblage* for Kunstmuseum der Stadt Wels, Austria, with Hans Knoll, Vienna, and a group of these works, and *Fluid Sheet Constructions*, for exhibition at the Rudolfinum, Prague.

1996 Builds *Box Trough Assemblages* and mass works of 1968-69 with Akira Ikeda, Tokyo.

1997 At Felletin, completes fabrication of tapestry for Notre-Dame-du-Bourg, Digne.

1998 Builds *Internal Measuring Rod for Room* (1965) with Galerie Potocka, Krakow in association with the Museum of Modern Art, Niepolomice; inauguration of the liturgical furnishings, including fenestration and tapestry, for Notre-Dame-du-Bourg, Digne.

1999 Completes model of tapestry conceived for Le Dorat, collegiate church, France, fabricated by Marianne Caron.

2000 Builds two *Metrical (Romanesque) Constructions* (1985) with Dorothea van der Koelen, Mainz for exhibitions in Basel, Mainz, and Münster (Westfälisches Landesmuseum).

2001 Builds with Steven Oliver *Carved Systems in Involution (Sculpture for Catrina Neiman)*, concrete; guesthouse designed by Jim Jennings, Oliver Ranch, Geyserville, California.

Builds with Dorothea van der Koelen *Conic Plane of 13 Masses and 2 Scales (with Elliptical Cut Hole)* (1972) for private collection, Freiburg.

Builds *Field Phalanx* (1964) for exhibition at the Lokhalle, Göttingen.

2002 With Matthew Tyson makes group of woodblock prints called *Alten I, Color* and *Alten II, Black*.

Artist-in-residence, University of California at Berkeley, Consortium for the Arts.

2003 Major exhibition organized by the Musée d'art contemporain de Montréal in collaboration with the National Gallery of Canada, Ottawa.

David Rabinowitch's biobibliography is available on the web site of the Médiathèque du Musée d'art contemporain de Montréal

www.media.macm.org